Our Stars Still Shine
Pet Memoirs of Love, Grief, and Hope

BookBaby
7905 N Crescent Blvd
Pennsauken Township, NJ 08110
www.BookBaby.com

First published in the United States 2022

ISBN: 978-1-66785-807-4

Our Stars Still Shine
Pet Memoirs of Love, Grief, and Hope

Rheanna Rasico

To Lady –
You are my greatest achievement and deepest sorrow. This is
for you, my darling. Love you forever and always.

Acknowledgments

First and foremost, I am grateful to the one who inspired me to create this book from the very beginning, my beloved soulmate, Lady. She was instrumental in the way I perceived life and love and continues to be even after her passing. Her life was a magnum opus, and I am honored to have played a part in it. There are not enough pages to write all our memories and moments, but they're inscribed in our souls. It was a gift. All of it.

I'm grateful to my husband, Andy, who never stopped encouraging me to write and go after my dreams. He is the sunshine of my life who gives the best hugs when I come home every day. Thank you for knowing when I needed space during the tears of writing and remembering, and when I needed to be held. I love you forever.

This book wouldn't be here if it weren't for the brave authors who contributed. What started off as a dream, quickly became a project that grew into focus. I'm so proud of each one of you for doing the hardest thing any pet parent can do – remembering the moments we said goodbye. Your stories inspired me, made me weep, and changed me. Thank you for blessing me. Our babies will forever live on as their stories resound in us, these pages, and in anyone who reads them.

Introduction

This book started its creative unfolding three years ago as a mere idea after I lost my own soulmate, Lady, and quickly developed into something fathomable. After collaborating with like-minded humans who shared the same vision and pain, the stories started pouring in; I was blown away at the outpouring of interest while blessed by their support and love. This book was delayed several times as I navigated through my own pain over the years as I additionally lost my dear brother two years after Lady passed, but this book quickly became a place of healing and gave meaning to that pain.

It is my intention through this book that our soulmates will always be remembered while providing comfort and validity to anyone who may be facing similar loss. We may be heartbroken our fur babies are gone, but we know their love lives on in us, our memories, and those whose lives were touched by them.

This book was written with love and tears from many different authors located worldwide. Each author has a different writing style and intent to their story; it is my hope that you hear the heartbreak and feel the love from each through their own words as they recount some of the happiest and most painful moments of their lives.

Thank you for reading our stories.

Note: Some names in this book have been changed for privacy.

In Memory

Lady	Teekee
Sage	Day-z
Libby Lou	Jacoby Joseph
Kody	Princie
Jesse	Tabby
Leo	Paulie
Zoey	Cricket
Bullwinkle	Beau
Twister	Rascal
Milo Allowishious	Hannah
Scamper	Rustler
Dexter	Angel
Brandy	Sunny
Stormy	Heidl
Bosco	Dixie
Maya Barralis	Pipi
Dede	Daisy
Maxie	Music Moreno
Porter	Izzy
Vespa	Kanook
Isabella Rose	Shasta
SoCrates Kan	Sebastian
Brandy	

My Sun, Moon, and All My Stars
By Rheanna Rasico

Death had thrown a grenade down my throat. What's left is a destroyed and shattered version of who I was. It's all savage—loss, heartache, everything. Grief has taken over. I look in the mirror, and all I see is a carcass looking back. I am gone inside because she's now gone. Our souls were the same. Where there was life and color, it is just a dark chasm of emptiness, sucking more and more life into the void of another dimension I cannot exist in, at least not fully. The life I know is over. I'd become a person I no longer knew or recognized, I am outside my body looking in, and I'm frightened at what I see. I've become the person I never thought I'd be. I experienced lows I never knew existed. I crossed mental barriers I never imagined I'd cross. It was easy. The ability to be nothing was…effortless. It moved in like it knew its way around. Snaked around my mind and spirit, caressed me like a lover.

I always thought the hardest part about losing someone you love is the losing part, but really, the hardest part is *everything*. It's the losing, the enduring, and ultimately, the realization that you are in a permanent place where you have forever changed. There's no getting out; there's no refuge. You are in the middle of an ocean, and there's no lifeline.

Things will never, ever, ever be the way that they were. I have lost my very soul. I often find myself surprised that the sun still rises, even after she's gone. How does life go on when such tragedy happens, when so much pain exists? The sun becomes a traitor to all who have lost.

To know her story, you must first know mine.

We moved to Wisconsin when I was three. It was a beautiful log home on a river. My dad designed and helped build it. Our log home was on two acres of property tucked far from our quiet street. Our back yard was spacious with the lawn ending where the grassy fields began. We created and maintained a trail leading down to the river for easy access. At the border separating the lawn from field, there was a tall tree that would have been the perfect tree house. I remember climbing that tree as far as I dare; looking out through the branches I could see all the way to the river and beyond. Sometimes I'd imagine myself as an orphan, alone in the world trying to make my own way. An expert at survival and climbing trees, finding my way through forests and scavenging for food. Then I'd hear my dad whistle from around the house, I could picture him standing on our front porch with his thumb and index finger in his mouth. It was dinner time. My imaginative story vanished as quickly as it came, and I was scrambling down the tree, jumping off the last limb and landing in grass and twigs. I would run diagonally to the left, across the lawn, and up the back porch steps, through the sliding door. I was instantly in our breakfast nook and took a seat at our oval table, big enough for a family of six. I sat with my back to the sliding door. My brother, Shannon, sat to my left, with my mom at one end of the table to my right. In front of me was my other brother, Nicholas, and next to him was my sister, Tiffany, followed by my dad at the other end. That was how we sat until we grew up.

I spent infinite days at the river, digging up old clams and funky-looking rocks. To the right of my house were vast open fields I'd often find myself running in, going on for acres and acres, collecting goldenrods and Queen Anne's lace, examining milkweed and the chrysalides attached to them.

Towards the back of the field, there was a shallow wood that hid a rusty car that had experienced more years than I. It had been demolished, the glass missing from all windows, doors dented, hood smashed, leaves and twigs were covering the blue leather seats. I always wondered about it, what was its story, and how did it end here. A river on one side and a dead-end street on the other. I never did find out.

Across the street from our house was a large stretch of land, but beyond that was a massive stretch of woods, it seemed like it went on forever. We'd spend hours upon hours in there, making our complex forts. Some of them were so extensive, we'd create rooms and even sweep the "floor" and keep things tidy. We made the most riveting story plots. Meanwhile, exploring deeper and deeper within the woods. I listened to the trees talking; the creaking of their branches as they gently swayed against others – forming a dance – the wind blowing through. I'd hear them, singing deep from their soul. I'd stare at the floor of the earth and be in awe of my existence and the mass of these magnificent beings. They frightened me as equally as they inspired me.

Some of my most transcendental childhood memories include sitting around the bonfire surrounded by family and friends; sky ink black, lit by the embers floating into the night. I'd watch them float away as far as I could see, gray smoke twirling and swaying from the wind. I would ponder the world's mysteries and think, I can't believe I'm here in this life, I can't believe I'm alive.

Ever since I was young, I felt I was an unusual child – on my own journey. I had always had friends, but never felt that deep girly-girl connection that I imagined I should – slumber parties every weekend while taking turns braiding each other's hair, makeovers, and midnight pizza. Maybe it was unrealistic. Animals and nature became my connection and they allowed me the space to truly be me. Later in life, I discovered I was an empath which helped me to finally feel comfortable in my skin and accept me for me.

When I was 11 years old, we moved almost an hour northeast, to another small town in Wisconsin. Still on a dead end with neighborhood kids to play with, but not the open fields we were used to. We got our own rooms, which was a vast upgrade since I had had to share a room with my sister. The new home seemed meant to be, even the basement door had a cat door built in which our cat, Libby, instinctively knew was just for her. The yard was a third of an acre, vastly different from the open fields our dog, Sage, was used to running in – leaping through the tall grass coming home to the sound of our calling. The house was cozy, decorated, and we liked it. We didn't realize at the time how much our lives would change in that house.

I was 16 years old, in high school, and finding my way. My brother, Shannon, and I were still homeschooled, but were taking classes at a couple of local schools. Mine being private, his public. Though my parents wanted him to attend my private school, he was adamant he wanted to experience the public-school atmosphere. Like always, when he got an idea in his head, he couldn't let it go. Many times, I'd ride along as my mom dropped off or picked him up. I always felt strange leaving him there – he was such a soft and misunderstood soul. I feared he'd cross the wrong kind of teenagers and end up getting beat up. Even though I was younger than him, I worried about him often, and in return, he would protect me growing up in more ways than one, my protective bear.

We were close growing up, had the same neighborhood friends, spent the most time at home with our parents, same sense of humor and personality characteristics. Even after we became adults, many nights we'd stay up and watch movies with our mom. Those are some of my fondest memories.

In high school I started dating my first boyfriend. We were together for over seven years – on and off again. It would later take many years to fully heal from the emotional and psychological toll it took on me, but despite the broken pieces of my heart, many happy memories were made that I can appreciate and reflect on.

When I was a senior in high school, our family pet, Sage, was diagnosed with Cushing's disease, she was about 14 years old. Sage was a beautiful full-bred English springer spaniel and was trained in agility. She won many ribbons throughout her life and we all simply adored her. I'd only known her in my life, never had I known a day where she did not exist.

It was a cold winter morning when we saw Sage couldn't get up. She was curled in a ball and could barely move. We were heartbroken in every sense of the word – we knew we had to say goodbye. Before my mom and sister rushed her to the vet, we all said our goodbyes. Sobbing with tears streaming down my face, I gave her all my love. How do you even say goodbye to someone you've loved your entire life? Knowing you see her now, but in a matter of hours, she will be gone forever.
It was then that our cat, Libby, walked over to Sage and they slowly touched the tip of their noses together. They knew they were saying goodbye – not for forever, but for now it was farewell.

After they left the house, I cried and screamed into my boyfriend's chest. I had never felt so much gut-wrenching pain until that point in my life. I was devasted – we all were. I chose not to go with them. I couldn't…I absolutely couldn't. I wanted to remember Sage how she was, and not as she passed. She had my mom and sister by her side the entire time, whom she loved the most, and they showered her with all the love as she left this life. She knew she was fervently loved as part of our family. Her passing changed us all and we never let her memory be forgotten.

A few years later when we were in college, my boyfriend adopted a border collie and black Labrador mix rescue puppy. One of his friends had a dog that unintentionally had a litter, so he volunteered to adopt one of the puppies. When my boyfriend brought his little boy over, I could see the pride that radiated from his soul. That puppy was simply adorable and entirely loved. He was all black with white markings on his chest, and tender eyes. I loved him like he was my own. He was full of life and perfect.

Several months after my boyfriend's puppy arrived, I started to feel a tug in my heart to find my own. It felt like something was calling me – but I didn't know where or who it was. I followed that tug and looked far and wide to answer the voice that was calling in my heart. *I'm coming.*

Growing up, I'd always loved the movie *Lady and the Tramp*. Lady's calm demeanor and effortless sophistication inspired me to find a dog like her. I knew in my heart my little girl was already named Lady Anne, I only had to find her. Hoping for a smaller dog that could snuggle and fit in my lap, like a cocker spaniel, just like Lady.

I so vividly remember searching on our family computer. Browsing rescue websites every night for the right dog, the one already in my heart. I inquired about several dogs, but for some reason or another, it didn't work out or they were already adopted.

At one point, I saw a beautiful King Charles spaniel rescue that seemed like a good match. She had golden and white colors with a kind face. However, her foster mom informed me the dog had been abused and needed special care. The dog was extremely suspicious of strangers. I felt I was up for the challenge, but in the end that didn't work out either. The foster mom was very hesitant and careful, as she should be, and I wanted to respect that beautiful animal. I wasn't in a place in my life where I had the resources to care for such a wounded soul. I kept searching for the one in my heart.

Finally, I found her. I had knocked on so many doors of opportunity and chance to only be let down, discouraged, unable to find the one in my heart, until now – until this moment. The door swung wide open and everything inside of me clicked with a momentum that could have made the sun and stars shine forever. I found the one in my heart, I found the very depths of my soul in the eyes staring back at me. This was the beginning of everything and for the first time in my entire life, I felt an instinctive change in the neurons of my brain. From that moment on, I became a momma…*her* momma.

I sat staring at the screen. This stunning black puppy, whom they named Black Cutie, was laying on her belly with her head on her paws, simply looking back at me. I read her description repeatedly. It said she was part black Labrador and cocker spaniel, which was perfect and everything I wanted. Her hair was crimpy and curly in the most endearing ways around her face and floppy ears. It was just a photo, but something in my heart clicked and the connection was instantaneous. She was mine and I knew I was hers.

I immediately wrote to the foster mom, inquiring if this puppy was still available and what the requirements were to adopt her. I literally couldn't stop thinking about Black Cutie. She was always in my thoughts, and I started to become anxious, I wouldn't rest until I had her in my arms and knew she was mine.

Her foster mom wrote back quickly and informed me she had just listed this puppy the same night I had written to her. By some miracle, I was the first one to inquire about her, as five other people after me requested her as well. I never am this lucky. Despite given the first say in the adoption, I still felt so anxious; it didn't seem possible that something so precious and beautiful could be mine. I was constantly worried they would give her to someone, despite their reassurances I had first choice. I lived in Wisconsin and Black Cutie was in St. Louis, Missouri. I was up for the drive and would do anything in my power to pick this little girl up and wrap her in my arms, but the constant fear that they wouldn't want to wait for me to drive down constantly rippled in my head.

Black Cutie's foster mom and I finally spoke on the phone, and it felt like everything was falling into place. She talked about Black Cutie's personality and birth order, and what type of breed she was. It was then that I found out Black Cutie was now assumed to be part black Labrador, border collie, and chow chow. She was the only black puppy from her litter as the rest of the litter were brown puffs that looked more like chow chows. Black Cutie was the only one that looked like her mom, who was a black Lab and border collie mix; all black with white markings on her chest. The father was allegedly a chow chow. I knew this meant she would grow to be a bigger dog than I had expected, no longer a lap dog in my future, but I loved her with my soul already and I didn't care. It was too late to have size be a factor; my heart found its song.

Black Cutie was scheduled to be spayed, so we agreed I could pick her up in a few weeks after she had healed. At that point, my boyfriend, mom, and I would then drive to St. Louis to pick her up. I was beyond elated and marked it on the calendar hanging in my room – the countdown had started for my very own, my Lady.

Before the day arrived for us to leave for St. Louis, I went to Petco and picked up things I thought a puppy would need or at least enjoy. I bought her a pink blanket, a tiny purple elephant, and a braided rope for future games of tug of war. I even got her a special collar and bandana – she was going to be adorable.

The day finally came to pick up my little girl. It was a Friday when we packed up the car with Lady's new toys and blankie and picked my boyfriend up for the drive down. The whole drive down, I couldn't rest or trust that she indeed was mine until I saw her in front of me and held her in my arms. I was on a mission to find my baby and bring her back. Such an incredible amount of unexplained anxiety grew inside my heart. Irrational and unsubstantiated, but there.

The next day we left our hotel to visit the St. Louis Gateway Arch before picking Lady up, we had a little time to spare. Though, the whole time I was only thinking about her. I just wanted to hurry up and get back in the car, I wanted her in my arms. We were so close. I still vividly remember us being there, walking up to the entrance, the cement walkway, through the doors and walking past the gift shop. People. There were so many people. We were crammed into the tram car, watching the floors disappear beneath us through the small window in the door. We got to the top and I remember walking around, feeling the arch move beneath my feet from the wind. My boyfriend and I snapped a selfie by the windows and eventually, the three of us left.

We finally headed out to Petco to pick up Lady as her foster mom was having an adoption day at that location. I remember the automatic doors whizzing open for me as I speed-walked to the back of the store; my boyfriend and mom were behind me as I outpaced them. A woman was sitting behind a table with a big dog cage sitting on the floor next to her. I saw a black puppy sleeping, all curled up. My Lady. I quickly told the woman sitting in front of me who I was, that I was the one adopting Black Cutie and the adoption fee had already been paid. She stood from the chair and crouched down next to the cage door, she gently pulled out my Lady girl and handed this ball of black fur mixed with crimpy curls to me. Lady was groggy from puppy sleep, but I wrapped my arms around her, held her to my chest and everything inside of me fell into place as all the anxiety and worry of losing her melted away. She was finally mine and I was forever hers. I relished in this moment of certainty and bond between us that I could never fully put into words.

There was another dog there waiting to be adopted. It was Lady's mom, Sweetie. Lady and she looked so much alike, except Lady's hair was longer and crimpy in certain places, whereas Sweetie's hair was short and flat like a typical Labrador.

Before we left, I let Sweetie say goodbye to Lady. We petted Sweetie and gave her as much love as we could. Sweetie laid on her back and let us pet her belly. She still had stitches from just getting spayed after her litter was born. She was incredibly gentle. To this day I regret not adopting them both. We then said our goodbyes and headed to the car as I held Lady in my arms. The three of us adored her as we all wanted turns of snuggles and kisses.

She was the best puppy on the way home. She slept almost the entire way, all snuggled in the backseat with my mom and me. We all couldn't believe how well she traveled.

After we dropped my boyfriend off, it was about dinner time when we finally got back home. My brother Shannon and dad must have been watching for us because as soon as we pulled up, they came walking out of the garage to see our new addition to the family. Lady was awake at this point and wasn't on a leash. She saw my brother and dad walking toward her, so she trotted up the driveway to greet them. She laid on her back in the middle of the driveway so they would pet her belly, just like her mommy did in the pet store. Lady would continue this throughout her life – she loved her belly rubbed.

As a puppy, she naturally loved chewing on anything that resembled a shoe, especially if it had a stiletto heel – the perfect size for her mouth. Many pairs of shoes were ruined during that stage, but I didn't care. I even kept a pair to this day that she chewed on, they still have the teeth puncture marks by the heels, a memory of such a fleeting stage in her life.

Even as a puppy, I took her everywhere whenever I could. Of course, there were times I couldn't take her with, as a young adult commuting to college, work, and when I went out with friends. My parents watched her while I was at classes or work, but for the most part I'd take her everywhere. She came with me to local baseball games, car rides, and different dog parks – she was my overwhelming sense of joy.

Eventually, my boyfriend and I called it quits and through it all Lady stuck by my side. It was a very difficult breakup; I ended up taking a semester off school as my depression was crippling and affecting my academics. I was already a tiny girl at 5'7", weighing 123lbs, dropping down to about 115lbs. I couldn't eat, I never felt hungry. When I did eat, it had to be soft foods – anything richer or heavier made me sick. However, I didn't let that stop me and I went back the following semester and took summer classes every year to make up for lost time until I graduated.

Since the first night Lady came home, she always had the option of laying on beds or couches. We were not the kind of family that made dogs sleep on the floor. Our couch and bed were good enough for them too. Our animals were everything to us and I enjoyed the calming and snuggly benefits of sleeping with my girl. At the time I had a twin bed which didn't leave much room for her. But starting from a puppy she'd sleep in between my legs, curled in a ball. As she grew, she still slept between my legs, often using my leg as her pillow, or stretching out her legs over mine. No matter what, she always had to be touching me. Always. Wherever we were – in the car, on the couch, bed – she always had to have her paw or head on me.

Lady was a very sensitive and emotional dog. We would always say she wore her heart on her sleeve as her facial expressions revealed exactly what she was feeling. She was the kind of dog who couldn't ever be yelled at. She had a soft heart and just needed to be talked to, she truly understood. With the expressions she gave, it was truly amazing to understand what she was feeling just by paying attention to her. Whether she was smiling and happy, concerned with brow furrowed, or sad with devastated eyes, it helped me understand her and be able to communicate and cater to what she needed.

Lady would sometimes get separation anxiety in specific situations. Inside our home she was fine, she knew that as her territory and safety zone. However, she had to know what room my mom and I were always in. It was a relief to Lady when my mom and I were in the same room, her job just got that much easier. You could tell from her face and behavior that she loved it when we three were together. Though Lady knew I was her mom and we absolutely adored each other to the extent that our sun, moon, and stars rose to each other's name, Lady also adored my mom and knew her as Grandma. If my mom or I left her in the car to quickly run into the store, or if we were both with Lady on a walk or out camping and one of us left to use the showers, Lady would cry and be on full alert for the missing one to come back. She would stare in the direction she last saw one of us go and as soon as she saw one of us again, she would start crying and jumping in excitement. We had to all three be together. We had a special bond that was not shared by any other.

Birthdays have always been a big celebration in my family and Lady's was no different. For her, we'd make it an all-day affair by going for a walk at her favorite park. We'd take our time, walking wherever she wanted to go, smell the smells, feel the water wrap around her legs as she waded into the creek. The long hair on the back of her legs floating in the water. She usually would run up ahead of me, but rarely ever went out of sight completely. She would stop and look back to make sure I was still following her. "It's ok, I'm right here," I'd say, and off she'd trot again. If there was ever a time when I was out of view – a tree or bush blocking – she'd immediately start trotting back to find me. She'd see me behind the tree, tail wagging, and give me kisses. She was truly devoted, but even more so, she was thoughtful and aware.

I usually had a towel waiting for her in my back seat as her hair was so kinky and long, it would just be dripping wet if I didn't wipe her down. Even when I did, she would just stand there calmly and patiently until I was done. She never ran off or was squirmy. She was always perfect, always did as was told, and always stayed by my side.

The next phase of her birthday consisted of visiting as many pet stores as possible. This girl *loved* her Petco stores, and I mean LOVED them. She knew exactly where her treat and food aisles were – I'd let her lead the way in the gentle way that she did. After all, this was her store, not mine. If she wanted to look at the fish and smell the cat litter, who was I to tell her no? I'd buy her favorite treats and a bone or toy. She wasn't really interested in bones, except in hiding them. She rarely chewed on them, ever. I always felt the bones gave her more anxiety than thrill, as she was searching for a hiding spot – bone hanging out of her mouth like a cigar – she would whimper and cry as if she just couldn't find the right spot in the house. Usually, she'd bury it in our bed, between the couch cushions, or in my husband's laundry basket. It was entirely endearing but I always felt for her during that stressful process.

On one of those birthday excursions, I bought her a pheasant toy. She was never really into toys, she loved human interactions like tug of war or chase, her favorite. It was cute looking with its gray-webbed feet, striped tail, and red and green patches on its face. It made the funniest sound, a low-pitched call like a cow who'd run a marathon. For some reason, she *loved* this pheasant. We'd play tug of war, fetch, or even some good old-fashioned chewing. Figuring *pheasant* was too long of a word, I just referred to it as a *duck* to her. Some days during playtime, I'd tell her to go get Duck. Sure enough, she'd come back wagging her tail with Duck hanging from her mouth.

We'd end the day with a special dinner for her – I learned I couldn't give her a birthday candle or sing Happy Birthday, as she would get scared and hurry upstairs. The candle smoke reminded her of fireworks my brother and I use to set off. It was never anything loud or intense, more sparklers and small cherry bombs that snapped when they hit the ground. She was a girl that didn't like loud noises – I respected that, I didn't either.

After her first four years of life, her fur coat started to grow thicker, wavier, and a mane started to frame her face. Most likely from the chow chow side of her, including her purple spotted tongue. But it always amazed me how she continued to grow and develop, even as an adult. I loved seeing her change as we got older together.

Of course, she wasn't a lap dog, but she wasn't as large as a Labrador either. She clocked in at 50-55 pounds, small enough for me to pick her up for a photo or mommy snuggles, and big enough to feel I'm hugging a life-size Teddy bear. My husband accurately called her Princess Fluff. But during bath time she shrunk to half her size.

Being a lap dog is just a state of mind. To Lady, she belonged in my lap whether we were both passengers in the car or while I was behind the wheel. Knowing how dangerous this was, I would shift her over to the passenger seat if I could. One afternoon I was driving back from running errands with Lady. Driving through our small town, I slowed down nearing an upcoming intersection when a police car coming in my direction saw the situation going on in my car. Lady's head was out my window with her butt smack dab on my lap. He gave me a good honk as I quickly hushed her to the passenger side, expecting for him to turn around and flash his lights. He never did.

She soon figured out she could stay in my lap during car rides if she laid in my lap - perfectly hidden from view. She'd put her head on my armrest, fully content, and fall asleep. If she wasn't in my lap, she would faithfully be on the passenger seat next to me, usually with her paw on my arm or we'd hold hands. She always had to touch me – if I wasn't already petting or holding her paw, she would remind me of our ritual by pawing my arm. Every single time. The older we got together, the more consistent this became. This not only happened every car ride, but it happened during the entire ride. Our car trips became a special bonding time for us; windows down, hair blowing, sunshine on our faces – looking at each other with smiles and complete trust – it was our time together to slow down, just us against the world. "I love you too, Lady." I'd say, mindful of the conversation we were having with our hearts.

Every year my mom and I road trip to a different state, making one big loop through it. Taking in the sights and sounds of people and places we'd never seen before. We make quite the adventure of it. Usually, we start planning a year in advance. We look at travel resources, scour the internet and create an itinerary in our designated travel binder. Looking through the state travel magazines, we circle cities or activities we want to throw into the pile of possibilities while out there. By the end of our review, the magazine is doggy eared with highlights and scribbles inside. We love to travel together, it's all about experiencing life's adventures – never missing a moment. This philosophy helped the three of us become incredibly close. Naturally, I always wanted to bring Lady with me. But most of the time it just wasn't possible for trips to states further away. There's no possible way I'd leave her with a stranger while I whitewater rafted or toured an underground cave. Knowing she's safe at home calmed my anxiety – though I always wanted her with me.

However, we were able to bring her along on several road trips to Michigan and our greatest trip together, to Minnesota. That is the trip I think of with the fondest memories. We packed up the van with our six-person tent, cooler, duffle bags, and of course, Lady had her bag filled with her food, leash, collapsible water bowl, and her own bed. Though to be honest, she rarely ever used it. Every night she'd want to sleep between us on the air mattress.

Lady didn't like missing out on anything, even while on car rides. It was just accepted that whoever was in the passenger seat would also have Lady on their lap. Not necessarily by choice, but by Lady's pure determination. We just accepted our fate, happily. Lady wasn't a small dog; she wasn't huge either. But at 50 pounds, long legs, and an immense amount of fur, we knew we'd have a Lady butt in our face pretty much the entire time while she craned her neck out of the window to have her own adventure. When she'd get tired of the fresh air, she'd curl up in our lap as best as she could and rest her head on the middle console. I can't imagine how that was comfortable, so I started putting my pillow there instead so she could sleep soundly with comfort. She was my baby and whatever she needed I would give her. She had my heart and soul entirely and unconditionally. It was so amazing to be able to experience that trip with her. We all felt a shared sense of freedom and adventure that stays with me to this day.

Often during the trip, Lady would be so exhausted from our full day of hiking or exploring, that she'd paw at me to come to bed. It wasn't nearly bedtime yet, but I understood she was tired. On one such occasion, she pawed at the van door. I had never seen her do this before, but curiously I opened the door. She hopped in and instantly curled up on a seat and fell asleep. I left the door open for fresh air and her freedom to leave. Other times on the trip, she'd paw at the tent. Yet again, I'd follow her request and unzip the tent door. She'd walk in with a mission and curl up on the bed to fall asleep.

This girl had her own thoughts, wishes, desires, and wants. She knew exactly what she wanted when she wanted. There was no doubt in my mind that she was conscious of her life, of me, of us.

One of my favorite memories of our Minnesota trip was visiting Temperance State Park. It was massive and endless. I remember walking up rocky cliffs while staying as far away from the edge as I possibly – holding on to Lady's leash tightly. She loved it with no fear or worry, she wanted to be ahead of us off leash like we normally do for our walks at home, but this wasn't like back home. We came to the beautiful river and walked on the edge, put our feet in, and made balancing rock structures. Lady beelined to the water and plopped herself in, laying with her back legs spread behind her, as the cool water flowed around, she lapped it up with her pink and purple tongue. Life was good. In this moment, everything was perfect, and nothing could penetrate this bubble of balance, safety, and joy.

We never left Lady alone or stranded in the car. We just would never do that to her. She would get anxious whenever she was separated if one of us needed to use the bathroom facilities while she waited with the other. She'd wait while never taking her eyes off where she last saw us, crying for the other to return. Seeing the missing person come out of the bathroom, she'd start jumping and crying, wagging her tail with the deepest devotion only to fully relax after she'd had her fill of belly scratches, kisses, and words of affirmation. She did not like it when we were separated and found comfort in knowing where we both were at all times.

Shared experiences tend to bring people together, a mutually shared moment can be emotionally and even spiritually unifying. The journeys Lady and I experienced together, on the open road with the wind in our hair and the sun on our skin, it molded us together even more. We were best friends, and the older we grew together, we quickly became the blood and bones of soulmates.

An opportunity opened for me to go on a date with someone I'd crushed on for years, but the stars had never aligned. I finally had that chance, and I ran full force with it. Our first date was amazing. We had so much fun, and he seemed so different from other guys I'd been with. He was electrifying and exciting, so full of life. Our first date turned into a second and third. Before I knew it, we had been dating for six months and it was his birthday. At this point, Lady was six and we were inseparable. Everywhere I went, she was always there. I'd take her with me to visit my boyfriend, farmer's markets, shopping at home improvement stores, the list was endless.

Her favorite errands involved us going through a drive-thru, whether it be the bank or fast food, she had now come to expect a dog bone when we'd reach the service window. She'd crawl into my lap and peek her head out the window, giving them her sweetest face. Sometimes the worker looked nervous to give it to her themselves, I'd reassure them she was friendly as they slowly reached out with the dog bone to Lady. She was so good though. Slowly she'd open her mouth and gently take the bone and disappear in the car. It would always bring a smile to their face. She was such a princess who lived up to her name.

Knowing my boyfriend loved the music band, O.A.R., and that they were going to be at a concert hall not too far away, I surprised him with concert tickets for his birthday. This earned me girlfriend points and ended up being an amazing experience together. Towards the end of the concert, one of the things they're known for at a point in one of their songs is for fans to spray a deck of cards up in the air. Cards falling and landing everywhere like confetti from the sky. It was glorious and euphoric. Before we left for the night, I purchased a gray racerback tank with the words *I Want Peace* with a peace sign on the front. It quickly became my favorite which satisfied my inner hippy vibes.

About a year or so later, my boyfriend and I got engaged and started planning our wedding. The first detail I had set in stone was Lady was to be our flower girl. I scoured through Pinterest to find ideas, eventually settling on her wearing a delicate floral wreath around her neck. Months before the wedding, we'd practice at the church her walking down the aisle with my mom at the end. Lady figured it out very quickly and was so proud of herself for not only getting to go inside a church but to be a part of this strange routine of walking down the aisle with my mom at the end of it. On the day of the wedding, having my girl with me as I got ready was so incredibly special. To have her a part of this day was even more incredible and everything I'd ever hoped for. I always told my fiancé, you're not just marrying me, you're getting her too. We are a package deal, okay? He understood we were unbreakable and inseparable; he happily complied and fell in love with her too. He regularly walked her as well, but for some reason Lady would take both of us on different walk routines at our apartment building. When I tried to walk his route with her, she refused. We had to go on the designated route just she and I had always done together.

When the time came for her to walk down the aisle, she was ready to go, though surprised by all the people looking at her. Like me, she was also an introvert. She did so well and started walking down the aisle, guests were in love with her. The photographers took their pictures of her but had their flash on, which suddenly scared Lady. She thought it was lightning and started to walk back toward me. My mom had to come get her and walk her down herself. Poor girl. Lady stayed in the church during the whole ceremony, quietly laying or sitting on the ground, watching and bearing witness to her mommy getting married.

Lady had only known living in my parents' house with me, but she adjusted to apartment life well when my husband and I moved in together after we were married. Though it was a much different lifestyle than having a fenced-in backyard to herself, I think the apartment life had its perks for her as well. She got multiple walks a day to accommodate her bathroom needs and not having a fenced-in yard. She also would get dropped off every day at my parents' house on my way to work, and I'd pick her up again on my way home. It was a great arrangement as my mom missed her terribly after Lady and I moved out. Lady was cared for during the day and at her familiar home with someone she deeply loved, and my mom had her quality time with Lady, someone she also deeply loved.

After eight months of apartment life, we purchased our first home together. Lady adjusted well again to her new surroundings and loved her huge backyard. Our property juts up to a 40-acre prairie which became exploring grounds for Lady and me. We'd frequently walk together in the back, sit together and stare at the sky, the birds, and feel the wind.

When Andy and I moved in together, we used his bed for our room and my bed we put in our spare room for guests. My bed was what Lady was used to and we'd spent every night on together. So much so, that after we moved in together, I'd often find her curled up on our old bed. Sometimes if I woke up and Lady wasn't on the bed with my husband and me, I'd go to our spare room and she'd be on our old bed, curled up. It always tore at my heart a bit to see this. I didn't want her feeling alone or sad. Sometimes I'd lay or take a nap with her on our old bed, she always seemed so happy when I did this. It was just like old times together, her and I. Most nights, however, she'd stay with my husband and I all night, she'd always sleep between my legs, or she'd snuggle between us. Every Saturday, my husband and I would wake up and we'd invite Lady to come closer to the head of the bed. She'd wiggle her way and stretch herself out, front legs and back legs completely stretched out. She was almost as long as I was when she did this. We'd pet her unconditionally with morning snuggles and kisses, she'd wag her tail happily and give us kisses too.

She loved my husband fully. She loved my mom entirely. She loved me unconditionally. I was her momma, and she knew it. She had complete devotion to me and I to her. We were irrevocably committed; I had her back and she had mine. There was no guessing or hesitancy, we were crazy for each other. Our souls had intertwined. I could tell instantly what mood she was in, what she loved, what her triggers were, what made her happy, sad, scared, or anxious. She also knew me. Whenever I'd get sad or cry, she'd look at me curiously and cock her face, moving closer she'd sit right next to me and put her paw on my lap. *It's ok, Mom. I'm here.* I can still feel the pressure of her foot on my thigh.

It was around her fourth birthday that a heavy weight rested permanently upon my heart. I'd think of the years she'd lived thus far and compare to how many she roughly had left. I dreaded every new year upon us. I dreaded December. I dreaded New Year's. I dreaded April as it was both our birthday month. I didn't mind getting older, I just didn't want *her* to get older with me. Stay young. With every year passing, I knew it was one year closer to me losing her and that was unfathomable. We were always close, her and I, best friends. But as we got older together, it developed into something much deeper – even spiritually. We were soulmates. I felt our spirits were so wrapped together they had melded into one. Nevertheless, I took this opportunity to process what this meant and how I could make every day of our life together the most meaningful. We lived every day together like it was our last. We truly lived for every day. Every moment we spent together was intentional, observant, and full. We loved and enjoyed the same fundamentals of life. The sun warming our skin. The wind blowing our hair. The soft sound of birds in the morning or the way leaves flapped in the wind. I can remember days upon days that we would lay in the yard and just rest next to each other, taking in the sights and sounds and smells. The world was our oyster – even if we'd never travel the world together, we felt that we owned it. Despite the joys of our intentional and focused moments together, the weight of knowledge pressed heavily upon me. It seemed like I thought about it every day, to the point I felt I was obsessing. I hated thinking about it. I hated that I was mourning for her while she was still alive. *I couldn't bear the thought that one day I will have to live without her.*

In April 2018, the year after I got married, I was 29 and Lady was turning nine. For her birthday that year, I decided to hire a photographer to capture a mommy and me session – just her and I. I cannot quite explain it, but I'm so glad I listened to the voice inside my soul. I felt that I needed to capture our time together. I always took lots of pictures of Lady and me together. But this year, something was heavier on my chest than normal, and I needed to have us captured together. We ended up getting the sweetest photos of us together. She was such a good girl and did so great in front of the camera. When I kneeled on the ground in front of her, I put her paw on my thigh and she just kept it there until the photographer was ready to move on. One of my favorite images from the session, was when Lady was on a break so the photographer could get some headshots of me. I was crouching closer to the ground and suddenly Lady trotted into the frame and sat down to the left of me. The photographer and

I laughed, clearly Lady wasn't ready to be done. I reached over with my arms on each of her shoulders to bring her in a little closer to me. In the photo of that moment, Lady and I are both beaming. The look of pride on our faces just radiates. There is an incredible amount of happiness and joy that is felt in that one photo. Furthermore, it is an accurate depiction of our bond. We were proud to have the other, and so darn lucky – more than luck – it was meant to be.

For our first wedding anniversary, we decided to go camping up north in the Apostle Islands. He'd never been there before, and I wanted to be able to show him all the spots that I'd only talked about. I wanted to take Lady with me, something just tugged at my heart to take her. Like I really needed to do so. Everybody kept telling me not to.

"Just enjoy your time with you two."

"She'll be ok without you. It'll be easier this way."

After toying with the idea endlessly, getting anxious and a knot in the pit of my stomach about the idea of not taking her with me, I decided to leave her at my parent's house and just enjoy the time with my husband. My mom and dad did take good care of her. She was happy to be with them and everything was fine. But I will always regret that I didn't take her with us for a final family camping trip with her. I think of it now and it still leaves me with a sick feeling. I wish I had taken her. I wish I could have that week back with her, with us. I know beyond a shadow of a doubt that I should have not listened to everyone and just followed through with my gut. Always follow your sixth sense. Always.

A month after we got back from the camping trip, I had scheduled a photography session for us three this time. I again felt that I needed to document us as a family and to continue so for as long as I could. There was a photographer who lived almost an hour away, but I liked her style and it was close to the area we use to live at as kids, where we knew there was a great ice cream place for after. We were to meet at the photographer's house and take the photos in an area not far from her yard. Lady jumped out of the car, I let her leash go so she could smell and wander. She walked about 20 feet and instantly started squatting to go poop. I cringed inside, watching her poop in the yard of this photographer that we had just met seconds ago. At least Lady didn't poop on her porch. I ran to my car which usually had a poop bag – thank goodness I had an extra in my trunk. I thought, #*dogmomlife*.

It was a great session. Lady listened and sat next to us on the blanket when we needed her to. She seemed to stay closer to me during the session. I must wonder if she felt she needed to keep an eye on me. After all, who was this human with a black object coming close to her mom? Lady knew she was a part of our family, and she wore it proudly. As she wore her emotions on her sleeve, so evident it was how she felt about us and her role in our family.

I will treasure those photos forever. Both from her birthday and our family session. They are perfect in every way and capture our love and bond – our unshakable loyalty that no matter what comes our way, it will always be you and me, kid.

A couple months after our family photos, we were going to go on our annual day-trip river float with our friends. A time for everyone to have fun and lay in the sun as we floated down a river. My husband and I had gotten into a spiff and I wanted some space to cool off, so I slept in our spare room. Lady was ecstatic to sleep in our old bed again and we snuggled all night long. I will remember that night forever. The peace and calm I felt from feeling her body next to mine. The pressure of her weight against me eased all my anxiety. That would be the last time I would ever sleep with her again. Later the following day, I dropped her off at my parent's house so she could spend the night and they would watch her while we were on the float trip. I didn't like her being alone for long periods of time. She wasn't used to that and it wasn't fair to her.

The tubing launch point was only a couple of hours away from our house, so we left in the morning; knowing Lady was safe with my parents, people who loved her. We had a great float trip, so many laughs and memories, but even today it makes me sick thinking about how much fun we had, not knowing that the thing I grieved about for years was starting to come to fruition.

After the float trip, we stopped for dinner before we made the two-hour drive back home. On the way home, we encountered some major construction and detour, which delayed getting back tremendously. We wouldn't pull into our driveway till close to midnight and being exhausted from a full day in the sun I called my mom to tell her I would just pick Lady up in the morning. Of course she didn't mind, she loved her time with Lady – especially the sleepovers as Lady brought so much comfort.

My mom told me Lady still wasn't eating very much. This had been happening for the past week. At first, this didn't register any concern, as Lady had always been a picky eater. Especially at my mom's house, as my mom more often gave in to her pickiness and would feed her treats instead. Lady soon picked up on this holding out routine equated to treats instead. But this was different. Throughout the week I had noticed it too – she didn't want to eat her full meal. I quickly went to the pet store and picked up various kinds of wet food, bone broth, even goat's milk. She'd eat new brands, but then after eating wouldn't eat it a second time. I reached out to different vets, an allergist, the thought was Lady had acquired an allergy to a certain meat. I never in a million years thought something more critical had ascended upon us.

It was Sunday, the morning I picked Lady up from my parent's house after they babysat her for our river float. I knew something had changed. She seemed much weaker, slightly distant, and just not well. I brought her home and was consumed with fear and concern. I was supposed to go to a bridal shower brunch and just didn't know what to do. Should I go or see how Lady handles the day? My husband was staying home, so I asked him to monitor Lady; I'd only be gone a short time. Before I left, I found Lady in our spare bedroom, curled up on "our" bed. I went in there and asked her what she was doing in there, silly girl. She seemed so sad. I hate that I went to that shower. I hate that I didn't stay home.

After the bridal shower, I stopped at the store to pick up some more wet food for Lady. I was desperate to get her to keep eating. After I got home, Lady and I curled up on the couch together and we took a nap. I still remember I was on my side in a fetal position, and she was curled up in the nook of my legs, she had her head resting on my leg. My alarm went off and I had to go photograph a session for some friends of ours. I felt sick to my stomach – again unsure of whether I should reschedule the session, what if it's for nothing and Lady just has a virus? My husband said he'd watch her for me.

During the entire session, I had the worst knot in my stomach. All I could think about was her. I needed to get back to her. My baby wasn't well, and something was very wrong. I ended the session a little early and upon checking my phone, had missed calls and messages. I called him instantly. He told me she could barely stand so he rushed her to the animal hospital near our house. He said they were pumping her with fluids as she was dehydrated and was doing better. My heart was hopeful – this is good news. The doctor had performed an ultrasound but wanted to wait to give the results till I got there. My stomach in my throat again, knots again.

I still vividly remember this drive. I remember rushing on the interstate, passing slow vehicles. I remember my stomach was twisted and completely upside down. I was shaking and wanted to throw up. At last, I got to the hospital and was ushered into the exam room where my mom and husband already were. Pretty soon they brought Lady in from the back where she was receiving fluids. She walked in wagging her tail, so happy to see us all, she seemed much better, and I was a little relieved. Maybe that's all she needed. Lady laid next to me and I petted her the entire time, she fell asleep as the doctor came in.

By the look on his face, I knew it wasn't good. A look of medical professionalism with a dash of sympathy on his face because he knows what he's about to say is going to ruin my life. Our lives. He told us the ultrasound indicated she was internally bleeding. There was suspicion of cancer in her liver. Likely hemangioma sarcoma. A brutal and evil cancer. It was at this exact moment that something switched inside of me. I cannot explain it, other than a stronger part of me I hadn't met yet took over. I had to be strong for Lady. I looked over at her while the doctor went on. I petted her soft, long brown hair and noted how it felt in between my fingers. The look of her closed eyes as she breathed calmly next to me.

After much discussion, it was decided Lady was to stay the night and have surgery in the morning. They had to give her a blood transfusion during the night has her blood count was low (due to the internal bleeding), and they had to confirm if she indeed was internally bleeding. I broke inside, knowing I had to leave her there. She'd never stayed anywhere she didn't know before. This was new, strange. I didn't want her to think I'd abandoned her. I hated this and just wanted to wake up from this ridiculous nightmare. I petted her lovingly and told her how much I loved her, that I'd be back in the morning. I could not let her go. I watched as they walked her into the back room.

The hospital told me they'd call me during the night to tell me about the transfusion outcome. I turned my ring volume all the way to loud – not that I needed it as I was already a light sleeper and knew I couldn't sleep anyways. Regardless, I woke up to their call in the early hours of the morning around 3:00 a.m. They said the transfusion went well; Lady was tired but doing well. They would check her blood count in the morning and perform surgery immediately to assess the situation. Something good – I was a little hopeful but knew we weren't out of the woods.

The next morning, Monday, I called into work – a family emergency. I had been wearing the same clothes since yesterday. My black Nike running shorts and my *I Want Peace* tank top from the O.A.R concert. I drove to the animal hospital to give Lady a shirt of mine and my pillowcase, so she could have familiar smells around her. I drove home and await anxiously for the surgery to begin. I received a call that Lady was priority that day and they had moved her to the first surgery of the day. They were about to begin and would let me know what happened. It wasn't more than thirty minutes when they called again – I got a sinking feeling, knowing that was too quick. The surgeon told me normally they could remove the cancerous parts of a liver, but for Lady, it was all over. He said he counted at least 18 spots of cancer on her liver – there was no way to remove it. He told me they were going to stitch her up and conclude the surgery.

Another part of me died. I knew what this meant. There was no hope. Lady was terminal.

What happened next was a struggle between the hospital and me. I wanted to take Lady home, so she could peacefully pass in the comfort of her own home, surrounded by her family, with an at-home vet. However, the hospital didn't want me to take Lady home. They said they'd call when Lady was ready to be picked up. Hours passed with no call. I called again and they suggested I leave her there, that they had vets there that could put her down. No. Absolutely not, I said. I wouldn't let this go. Finally, they said we could come get her.

They let us in the back but told us she probably won't wake up – she was drowsy from the anesthesia and terribly weak. They weren't able to stop the internal bleeding, and it was just a matter of time.

I laid with her on her dog bed, in the back of the SUV as we were driven home. I petted her gently, as she drifted in and out of sleep, letting her know mommy was there with her. She wasn't alone.

When we carried her from the SUV I saw her nose wiggle, she was smelling the fresh air, though her eyes were closed. I knew that she knew she was home.

After spending several hours with her, laying outside on her bed with her, hearing the birds sing, and the wind blow – we brought her inside the house as it was getting dark.

Even though the animal hospital had given her another shot of pain medicine before she left, I didn't want her to suffer in her final moments. That wasn't meant for her – Lady deserved better. She had led an amazing yet self-less life. She deserved to be led into the next life with peace.

We called a mobile vet to come to our house that night. When she arrived, she examined my baby girl and told us Lady was ready to go. We already knew this but weren't ready to hear it.

From the time when we picked Lady up from the hospital to this very moment, I had talked with my baby for the entirety. I told her everything I ever felt about her. Everything I wanted for her, for us. How she was my sun, and I was a mere planet who was fortunate enough to get to revolve my life around her. That the incredible love I had in my heart for her did not compare to the vast expanse of the sun, moon, and stars combined. I thanked her for allowing me to love her, for sharing her beautiful life and soul with me, for loving me, and for giving me a chance to be her mommy. For believing in me when no one else did, for listening to all my secrets, for giving me strength when I had none. For everything, utterly everything. Everything, my dear. And it was then that I told her it was ok. It was ok to go. I told her to wait for me on the other side and that I'd love her for the rest of my life – I vowed she would never be forgotten but loved with every new day, in the sunrise, in the wind, in the flapping of the leaves on a tree, and in every sunset. I begged her to be at peace.

The vet started to slowly administer the final injection when I noticed Lady had stopped breathing. The doctor said that wasn't possible, she had barely been given any dosage. But I knew – a mom knows. Lady had left.

The doctor confirmed with shock what I already knew. She decided to still administer the rest just in case. I knew in my heart, Lady wanted to go on her own terms. And she did.

Lady passed away on Monday, August 13th, 2018. There was an open window right next to her and I'd like to think her soul slipped so quickly into heaven while listening to the birds chirping outside, feeling the hands of all her favorite people on her. My husband, my mom, my sister, and myself. On this day, I too died.

That night, my husband and I slept in the spare room. On Lady's and my bed, it made me feel closer to her. I remember crying all night with on and off again dreams of her not being truly gone. Only to wake up with a force of realization that hit me like a brick to the face. From then on, I slept with her pheasant stuffed toy. To this day, I still sleep with it in my bed. It brings comfort, having something of hers to clutch as I meet her in my dreams.

Every month, around the date of her passing, I display a fresh bouquet of flowers in our house. I keep her photos around and still haven't come to terms with cleaning out "her" drawer in our kitchen. It took me over a year to pack up her water and food bowl. It sat in the kitchen against the fridge just as she had last left it. I touched it delicately, before putting it in a special bin for safe storage.

I created a memorial for her on my built-in shelf – displaying her "Best Friend" water bowl, leash, cement paw impression, an intricate lantern in honor, and her urn with a beautiful landscape printed on the outside. Fitting for a girl that just loved being outside and to have as many adventures as her life would allow us.

The hours, days, and months that followed were gruesome and bitter. It has been the worst pain of my life. Family and dog-loving friends were understanding and sympathetic. Many gave me memorial items and sent cards and flowers. It was so considerate. But how do I keep going?

After a while, people on the outside started to wonder why I wasn't "moving on." Why I wasn't getting another dog. Why I was still sad. Because my process of grief didn't align with their timeline.

I had gotten to an all-time low. I hated myself, I hated life, I hated death, I hated everything. I was crying uncontrollably, leaning up against our dining room wall. My husband was trying to console me. I collapsed onto the floor with no strength. I made it to the bathroom somehow and locked myself in. I didn't want to live; I didn't want to die; I didn't want to exist. I wanted to just be with Lady somehow. I wanted to end it all gently, to slip away quietly – like I never was born. But we didn't have enough pills anyways. I begged God to just take me.

Let me have a heart attack from a broken heart. Just let my heart fail. My husband started banging on the door and managed to unlock it from the other side. I just laid prostrate on the floor of the bathroom. I'd fully and overwhelmingly given up.

Months passed. I was laying on the couch – the sun streaming through the floor-to-ceiling windows onto the blanket that covered me. I sensed the warmth and thought of Lady. My heart was mourning her. My whole body went numb and started tingling, starting from my lower body. I remember just staring at my legs, feeling paralyzed. I was perfectly still and quiet. Yet on the inside, I was screaming a maddening cry. I thought how odd, I can sit here perfectly still, and nobody notices me, they have no idea of the mania inside my head.

What I'm about to share, many people won't believe me, and that's ok. I don't need belief. I only write it because it's what happened. About six months after she passed, I started receiving visions of her. I'd never had anything like this happen before in my entire life. But there they were. The visions were sent to me and started to come more frequently.

The visions had the same characteristics which helped me separate them from dreams. They were only a few seconds long. They usually came before I'd fall asleep or I'd wake in the night to have one. During these visions, I had full control over my thoughts and body. I could feel myself in bed, the sheets over my skin. I could think during them and process information. I also could open my eyes, see my room, close them again and see the vision again. All the visions I had of her answered quiet questions I had in my head. What life was like for her? Was she happy? Where was she?

The first vision I received was of Lady in our hallway, I was calling to her – she looked happy. She then did a silly twist and jump as she disappeared into the wall. She was showing me she wasn't held by time and space anymore – she could go anywhere but was also around me.

Through the course of the year that followed, I received many more visions about her. One night, I had another terribly low moment. Lying on my side in bed, facing away so my husband couldn't see, I wept from my soul. With everything in me, I wished for an ending. To quietly slip away in my sleep. I prayed for this. I begged for this. It didn't happen. But instead, I received a vision that night that was the one that helped me heal and comforted me the most. The vision was of Lady in a beautiful and lush wildflower field. She was running and playing with my grandparents' dog, Frisky, who'd died before Lady was born. I can still picture her face – she was so incredibly happy, smiling, looking off to the side as Frisky was chasing her. It was then that I knew she was safe and happy. Though it hurt beyond comprehension to have her gone, it brought immense comfort.

A couple of years after Lady passed my brother unexpectedly passed away. The brother I was closest to – the sibling I had grown up with playing with neighborhood friends. The brother who also loved animals with every cell of his being. The brother who he and I would secretly talk in sign language and laugh at the same weird humor. He died on the cusp of his life blooming, his life taking off into something beautiful when he had overcome so much adversity in his life, more than what most people could ever comprehend. He was gone. His heart suddenly stopped, and if anything was left of mine at this point, it too had stopped. That night, I received a vision. It was of Lady resting in the wildflower field, her face turned, looking intently off in the distance. She was staring at something I couldn't see off frame. But then, in an instant, she ran off in the direction of her stare. I know and believe she saw my brother arriving in heaven. She ran to greet him. It brought much comfort, knowing they were together.

I've had many visions in total – they come and go in frequency, but I journal them as best as I can. I don't know why I've been fortunate enough to have them, but I'm beyond grateful. I'd like to think the bond Lady and I shared is still so strong, even in the afterlife she's able to connect with my soul.

Often with these visions, I'm not only receiving visuals, but I receive intuitive information; explanations or information that I otherwise would never find out. While receiving the vision, I suddenly become informed of specific things.

One night, I was missing Lady especially much while writing this story. My alarm woke me – time to get up for work. But I felt Lady. I literally felt her curled up beside my stomach as I lay on my side facing the closet. My body had even formed the perfect concave as I spooned her curled body. I felt the pressure of her body against mine. As soon as I became fully awake, the pressure of her body disappeared.

I'd like to say it gets better with time. But it doesn't. Death is permanent, and so often their absence screams louder than their presence. The rich moments of life, breath, and movement are replaced by the echoes of emptiness. However, the gift of time allows a smoothing over the pain. It isn't as paralyzing, but it is always there. A constant and quiet reminder. Time heals the sharpness of the pain, smoothing it over to be bearable and livable. The wound heals into a scar; no longer raw and vulnerable but always there. I may no longer feel her heartbeat or the warmth of her skin – silky brown hair splayed between my fingers as I had petted her – but I still feel our bond. The cord that connected us in life still vibrates between us after her death.

Life continues even when every second without her seems like a betrayal. Today, as I write this on a warm October Sunday. I sit in the same part of the living room where Lady left us. Different couch, different room color, but same spot. It's been three years, one month, and three weeks now since she passed. Though I've finally come to the point in my journey where I can talk about her without crying, I still cry about her frequently. I think about her daily; I miss her with every breath – my heart is always looking for hers. I can find happiness in my life again, but I will never be the same. I don't laugh or joke as much as I used to. I'm not as outgoing. I can't feel the once spark in my spirit. I changed forever when she left. Her death took with it the best parts of me; they were there only because of her. But it's ok. I'm comfortable with this. These new terms of life, this pain, they're all reminders that she was here. It helps me feel close to her. It is the price I pay for love. Pain is the cost to love and be loved.

It is a daily routine, this adjusting to life without her thing. I am in a better place now than where I was when I collapsed on the bathroom floor. But it's something I live with daily. My heart isn't the same; my body isn't the same; my life isn't the same. I am a survivor of this trauma because I have her love and memories to carry me through. I have the promise of seeing her again when the world decides to let me go. Handing me off from body to spirit as we fly off; my baby by my side just as it was, just as it should be.

Lady's life mattered to many. But it especially mattered to me. She was my very soul. She was my best friend, sister, confidant, and teacher. She still is, even though she's gone.

Her story deserves to be told and her life to be known and honored. She lived, breathed, laughed, loved, and changed many lives along the way. Writing her story was alone one of the bravest things I've ever done. Remembering the happy moments is still painfully sweet, but writing the difficult memories is excruciating.

In Lady's life, she camped throughout Minnesota, Michigan, and all over Wisconsin. She proficiently knew well over 50 words or instructions. She understood complete sentences and could differentiate between peoples' names. We watched more sunrises together than most people see in a lifetime. She could read facial expressions. We both loved ice cream (McDonald's Oreo McFlurry, sans the Oreo for her) and long walks in open fields. She loved belly pets and back massages. She loved laying down in rivers and creeks. She loved shimmying down hills on her back. She loved playing hide and seek. She loved me. I loved her.

My dearest Lady,
I did this for you. I did it for *us*. You are loved and missed, but daily you are remembered. In the way the leaves rustle, the colors of the sky, and the smell of summer mornings. You will forever be in those moments.

Thank you for sharing your life with me. During your life, you taught me how to be a mom with a fierce and protective love. Your absence taught me that love is the strongest thing in the universe. We truly lived every moment, every second to the fullest, leaving nothing to chance and no words unspoken. We took from life everything it had to give to us. The depth of appreciation and pride still evades all dimensions of time and physics. I feel our bond, strong and warm between us. I know you feel it, too, on the other end of this tie that connects us. Thank you for all of it, Lady. It was a gift.

An excerpt taken from the eulogy I wrote for my brother:
Though the ocean of grief is endless and vast, I become one with the ebb and flow of its strength. I submit myself to its changing forces. By your presence, I was changed, and by your absence, I will be changed. Grief is not a doorway; you do not just walk through and it is over. No. Grief is forever; it is a new life; the depth of changing and molding that occurs depends entirely on how you allow it. I choose to be changed for the better. I choose to be more like you, to love more, and to judge less. I will feel every fiber of this pain because you are worthy. I will grieve forever for you. For the years we never had and the moments never lived. Every second of pain is justified because your life meant the world.

Lady

Jesse: The Loyal and Loving Lab
By A.D. Valentine

There once was a litter of black Lab puppies. The smallest one, the baby runt, stood by his owner's side all of the time. No matter where they went, he was there just waiting to get a soft pat on the head. Inching closer and closer to being loved, he stood by their sides even when they had to get rid of him. A new family took him in; a husband and wife who had a wild, crazy, mutt-wooly dog of their own. This dog became his brother. Finally, a brother he would get to live the rest of his days with.

He stood by the family when they moved from house to house and ended up at a new house in the woods. He stood by his family when a wild cat from the woods showed up and nominated him as one of her doggy daddies. Loyal as ever, he never left the family's side. He and his new brother would go on lots of adventures together. Eventually, his family had a puppy of their own, a "human" puppy, a baby person who would eventually grow to be a child, who would then grow up too. As the loyal and most loving Lab grew up, sometimes his family fussed when he ate things he felt did not belong in his yard; occasional mops, brooms, sticks, birds, an armadillo, and even a possum. He remembered his training as a hunting dog from his life before he was adopted by his new family. Through the years, the human child grew to love him fiercely, and in return, he loved her, too. She reminded him of his human mama. Whenever they were outside playing in the yard, he would follow them both around.

The years rolled on. The small, human child grew into a taller human, and the loyal Lab and the dreamer dog grew into old, senior dogs. Time slipped by until both fur brothers grew old, their hips slow-moving and sore in the winter months. Their muzzles were sprinkled with white and gray. Eventually, the dreamer dog, his brother, went to sleep to have amazing dreams of being a puppy again. But this time, he didn't wake up. The loyal Lab was at his side when his master lifted his brother for the last time, carrying him off. Ever the optimist, he wagged his tail, still unflinchingly loyal to his family. As the next few years pressed on, he grew frailer. While he still longed for head pats and to follow his family on trail walks in the woods, one day, he did not feel like he could even stand. For the first time that day, he refused to eat, giving just three thumps of his tail. A way to say, *Thank you for caring for me, human mommy, but I just can't today.*

That night he cried out in pain and sadness, for he knew his time on earth was short. He did not want his mommy to be sad, but he knew that he would miss her when he went. Before the sun came up the next day, he would take his last breath and rise to meet his fur brother in doggy heaven. It is there he plans to wait, tail thumping at all the other dogs and cats there, steadfast as time goes on in the ever-optimistic expectation that one day, he might meet his human mommy, sister, and daddy. There, at heaven's gate, he will wait, the ever loyal and loving Lab, where he will snuggle and love his special humans once again.

Jesse

Kody, The Dreamer
By A.D. Valentine

Once there was a large litter of brown and black fuzzy puppies, born in rough conditions. The mamma wanted to take care of them all, but their owners were not caring for them properly. One of them, perhaps the smartest one in the bunch, dug a hole through the fence and went straight for the neighbor's house. It was the coldest day of winter, but that didn't stop the shivering, curious puppy from seeking shelter next door. He just knew he would find his forever home that day.

This puppy loved to seize each day of life. He believed in living to the fullest. Each day was an opportunity to live and love life. He dreamed of chasing and sniffing animals, he even dreamed of going to the vet. He was never afraid, either. A trip to the vet meant meeting new animals, sniffing more butts, and getting to play with the doctor. He never wanted to miss out on any life experience. He dreamed of playing, chasing, and trying to catch squirrels or birds but never managed to, he dreamed of playing with his owners, and tug of war with his toys. He was smart and knew every trick taught, even with just being shown only a few times. He was proud of that, too. He got along with all other animals, although for some he was just too much to handle, his energy and exuberance were catching. All who knew him could tell stories of this dreamer dog, which made them smile. He dreamed of seeing what was just on the other side of the horizon. He only began to slow down in his old age. During naps that lasted longer than before, he would dream of playing in open green fields of grass and meeting new critters at the park, as when he was younger.

One day, in his old age when his muzzle was snow specked in white, on another very cold day, he settled in for a long nap, dreaming of being a young, brown-bear puppy; chasing, yipping, frolicking through the woods, jumping in the lake at the park, and playing with his adopted fur brother, the loyal Lab, Jesse (whom he loved much more than he let on). On that day, he did not wake up. His dream continues even today, only this time, he is in heaven and young again just like he dreamed of. Dream on, sweet Kodiak (Kody).

Kody

Little Lion Heart, Lots of Love
By A.D. Valentine

Once there was a bunch of orange kittens born to a proud kitty mamma. One of those kitties was special. He had so much love. He loved his mommy, brothers, and sisters. When his new adoptive family brought him home, he learned to love them, too. He loved his new mommy; she even had ginger fur on her head, just like he did. He loved his new daddy. He loved his new sister. He loved his new home. He loved playing. He loved kneading all over the family's soft blankets with all four paws. He loved stuffed animals. He loved catnip on warm sunny days. He loved to eat. He loved lying on top of his mommy's chest. His purrs were so loud they would squeak and trill. He even learned how to say "*Ma Ma*" when he was hungry. He loved so many people and so many things. He loved his new human grandmother and grandfather. One thing he did not love was thunderstorms. The sound of crashing thunder was not a favorite thing for him. But he also loved to explore.

One night he heard a noise. The sound was just too good to pass up. He was so curious that he ran out the door, to a world he had never explored before. No one knows what truly happened. Perhaps he was defending his mommy and daddy from an intruder, or he saw something that looked quite fun to pounce on. Whatever it was, he was hurt. His family rushed him to the kitty doctor. But it was too much for him to bear. His little heart, so full of love, could not keep beating to keep him alive. The kitty doctor needed to make him sleepy to help him. But his sweet little heart, still so full of love, just quit after the doctor gave him medicine to sleep.

Although he is not alive, his little lion heart, because of his fierce love, will always be remembered, treasured, and sorely missed. The small-hearted kitten had a heart of gold. Live on in heaven freely forever.

Afterward:

One cc of blood. That is the amount moving throughout Leo's 14-pound adult feline body. This is the result of hypertrophic cardiomyopathy. This, combined with such an unusually sized small heart, is the official cause of death in our beloved little heart of gold lion. We love you, rest in peace.

Leo

Zoey, The Love of a Lifetime
By Andrea Cosmano - Forever and Always Zoey's Mom

Zoey. Her name means life. Little did I know at the time, how appropriate that name would be for her.

My mom and I had a holiday tradition. Every Christmas, even after I moved out and got married, she would buy me a dog calendar. It was in that calendar I first discovered Bernese mountain dogs. I was mesmerized by their beauty and striking markings, their loyalty, and the love they had for their person. It was at that point, that I knew this would be my next dog. After doing all the research about their life expectancy, health, temperament, and care, I began the search for a reputable breeder. After numerous inquiries and just about giving up, I decided to make one last phone call. I sat in the grocery store parking lot and dialed the number, expecting to hear the same response – no, we don't have any left. The phone rang three times before a lady answered.

"Hello?"

"Hi. I'm calling to inquire about Bernese puppies. Do you have any available?"

The lady on the other end stated she had one left. She described her as a sweet, loving, and confident little girl, but absolutely beautiful. I gave her my email address and she said she would send pictures. I saw my first picture of Zoey on

September 28th, 2009, and I knew I was in love. In those first pictures, the sunlight was shining all around her head and it appeared as if she had a halo. She was gorgeous and I knew she was my girl.

I picked her up on October 3rd, 2009. I was so excited. I didn't even sleep that night. I was out of the house and on the road by 6:00 a.m. My first Bernese mountain dog. I waited a very long time and I was finally going to have my very own. The first time I saw her she was sleeping peacefully with her little head tilted sideways between her paws. She was the last one left from her litter. Elaine, the breeder, picked her up and put her in my arms. Zoey was still groggy from sleeping and just looked at me with her sweet, little eyes. I sat down in a chair and she went back to sleep in my lap. She was the cutest thing I had ever seen. She was so fluffy and furry, she looked like a little bear cub. She was all black with some white on her chest, paws, and the tip of her tail. She had a white stripe down her face and two brown spots above her eyes. She had the biggest brown eyes and the longest eyelashes. Her little nose was all black and her little ears were so floppy. She was as soft as cotton and I couldn't wait to get her home. She was just perfect.

I placed her in a crate in the back of my SUV and we began the three- and one-half-hour drive home. It wasn't long after we left that she began to cry. I started talking to her in a very soft, motherly voice, but that didn't seem to help. As we traveled down the road, I began to smell a terrible odor and realized she had gone to the bathroom in the crate and was trying to get away from it. I pulled over on an exit and immediately removed her from the crate. She didn't have anything on her and was so happy to be out of the crate. I had some paper towels and cleaned it as best I could while still trying to keep her in the back of the car. At that point, I realized she would travel better by being closer to me, so I took some blankets I had brought along and put them with her in the front passenger seat. For a while, she was content and slept curled up in the blankets, but when she woke up an hour into the drive, she kept trying to crawl into my lap. After trying to drive and keep her in the seat, I finally gave up and she crawled in my lap, curled up and slept there the rest of the way home. My heart melted. It was at that point she had begun to wrap herself around my heart. Little did I realize, that was only the beginning.

We arrived at home around 2:00 p.m. By that time, she was ready to explore her new surroundings. I carried her from the car to the backyard and she met her Siberian Husky sisters and her dad for the first time. Sydney and Kalin were not quite sure about this little bundle of joy. They did the initial sniffing but ended up running from her as she chased them around. After a while, Zoey tired of that game and came and laid down in the grass by me. She put her perfect, adorable, little-black head on my leg and looked up at me with the most adoring, loving eyes; the little brown spots above her eyes moving independently with such expression. It was as if she was looking deep into my soul and at that moment I knew she was different, special. We had already developed a bond that I had never experienced before, something so unique and rare. I knew this precious little being would change my world, be my world, and it would never be the same again. I knew in that short period of time, she had become a part of my heart and I would do anything to make her life as perfect as it could be for as long as she was with me. It was then I promised her I would take care of her every need and I would never let her suffer. She gave me her heart and I gave her mine. From that moment, she was my Zoey, my princess, my perfect little girl.

I spent every moment, of every day and night thereafter, being with her and training her. Within a day, she learned to push her Kong around on the kitchen floor so her food would fall out. When she wasn't pushing her Kong around, she was with me on my lap in the kitchen. If she wasn't on my lap, she was lying next to me as close as she could get – there wasn't even an inch between us. Zoey was always a very gentle girl. Even during the puppy stage when she would bite, it was never hard. She would put her mouth on my hand or fingers, but never bite down. During all this time, I quickly learned how very smart Zoey truly was. I only had to show her how to do something about three or four times and she had it down. She mastered all the basic commands quickly, so I began to teach her commands by hand signals. Once again, she picked it up quickly. By Thanksgiving of 2009, she was sleeping with us in our bed. She had to be in between us, on her back, with her four paws up in the air. But more importantly, she had to be touching me. If I moved, she would move so she could continue touching me. She was my special girl.

Christmas of 2009, Zoey went with us to my parent's house for the day. She was five months old and my family could not believe how well-behaved she was. I, of course, took all the credit, but really it was all Zoey. She was so eager to learn and please me. It was about that time I realized how connected we had become. It was as if she was reading my mind and knew what I wanted her to do without even speaking words. She would look at me and just know how I wanted her to act. She was truly incredible.

Zoey had a wonderful life. She was a princess and that is how she was treated. She had a bright pink collar with a pink name tag outlined in rhinestones. She would even lay down with her front paws crossed just like a princess. She was the definition of spoiled. She didn't like to do most of the normal things dogs liked to do. She didn't play fetch or play with her dog toys. She didn't even like to go outside when it was raining or when the grass was wet as she didn't like to get her paws wet. She just loved to be with her mom and dad. Whether it was inside or outside, we always had to be in her sight, she always had to keep an eye on us.

Every night before falling asleep, her dad would give her a body massage. He would massage her legs, shoulders, paws, and her head. She would make snorty pig noises so we knew she was in heaven. Her favorite "treats" were strawberries and Brussels sprouts. Any time she heard the knife on the cutting block, she would come running and sit in the kitchen, patiently waiting for her treat. Whether it was broccoli, cauliflower, cucumbers, green peppers, watermelon, or berries of any kind, she always knew some would be saved for her.

No matter where I was or what I was doing, I was always thinking about Zoey. I didn't want to be away from her for long because I didn't want her to miss me or think I wouldn't come back.

Zoey's favorite time of the year was, of course, winter. She would get so excited when it would snow. She would go outside and begin turning around in circles. She would stick her face deep in the snow drifts and bite at the snow that had fallen on the ground. When she would remove her head from the snow, it would be covered and her face would be all white. She would just lie on the deck with the snow falling all around and look out over her kingdom. There would be times when her black fur would be completely white from the snow falling on top of her. She absolutely loved it! She was so well insulated, but the snow would not melt and there would be perfect snowflakes still intact on her fur. She was always so happy in the snow, tail wagging, so alert, so beautiful, and so majestic.

But Zoey just loved to be outside. She loved to chase the squirrels on the fence and the ones that had somehow gotten past her to the bird feeder. She would run off the deck into the yard barking at them to move along. She was able to see everything from her deck and nothing would get past her. There were times a bunny would end up in our yard and have babies. All I had to do was tell Zoey once to leave them alone and she would never go back by the nest. As I said, she was special.

We had a second home at Innsbrook, a three-season home in a gated community and we were there every weekend from March to November. This is where Zoey developed her love of deer and horses. As usual, Zoey quickly learned when we said, "merp-merp," a deer was around. She would run to the front door or one of the sliding doors and look out the windows to spot the deer. You could always tell when she saw one, as she would whine and bark. She would begin jumping up and down as if to say, "I see it, I see it, Mom and Dad. Thank you for sharing it with me."

We would take drives in the ATV and take her down to the stables to watch the horses. She was mesmerized by their immense size and again would whine when she saw them. I think she was surprised there was another animal bigger than her! One day she jumped out of the ATV and was quite surprised when she reached the ground how much bigger than her they actually were. One day, there was a very friendly horse by the fence that was as interested in Zoey as she was in him. He reached through the fence as Zoey walked up to him and they touched noses. It was a very sweet exchange that I caught on camera and is one of my favorite moments – a majestic horse meets my strikingly beautiful Bernese mountain dog. Her tail was wagging and she laid down on the ground next to me as I fed the horse some grass. She was never far from my side. My constant companion day and night.

That closeness was so evident when she would step on our flip-flops when we walked. She did it so often that we would turn around and look at her, "You walk on your feet, we will walk on our feet." She knew when she did it as the look on her face was, *I'm sorry mom and dad. I didn't mean to do it. I just love you so much that I want to always be as close to you as possible.* Of course, we never yelled at her and it got to be a joke. How could we be mad at something so precious and pure?

Then the day that I will never forget, September 3rd, 2018. It was Labor Day weekend and a normal day. Zoey was outside and as she tended to do when it's time to come in, she bounded from the bottom step to the landing without taking any of the four steps in between. I didn't think anything of it until she started limping a day later. By Tuesday, it had not gotten any better and I called the vet. This was just the beginning.

We arrived at the vet and I had them help me get her out of the car, so she didn't jump out and hurt herself worse. She was so happy – wagging her tail – wanting everyone to pay attention to her. Of course, that was the easy part. She always got attention no matter where we want. She was putting weight on her right, front leg, but still limping. We were taken to an exam room as we waited for the vet. Zoey was very uncomfortable as she did not like the vet, so I sat on the floor with her and stroked her head. She was panting from nervousness. The vet walked in and I explained what had happened. She wanted to watch Zoey walk, so she had us walk away from her and then back to her. She didn't notice anything with her gait, so she decided to take X-rays so they could get a better idea of what might have happened. They took Zoey in the back and brought her back about ten minutes later. It seemed like forever as I waited for her to return. The vet came back in and we looked at the X-rays. The first thing she said was there wasn't any cancer showing up on the X-rays, so at least we could rule that out. Cancer? Why would this be cancer? She hurt her leg running up the steps. This had nothing to do with cancer. The vet didn't see any break or fracture and thought she had just bruised it badly. She sent us home with meds, said she should be calm and relaxed and if it didn't get better, bring her back in a week. We got help getting back into the car and made our way back home. I was relieved and knew she would be better. She would just need to lay around for the next several days, that shouldn't be difficult as it was one of her favorite things to do. Still – the mention of cancer stayed with me and began to float around in my head. That horrible word, that terrible and dreaded word. But I wasn't too concerned. She would be fine in a few days and all would be well.

That week was very hectic as we began moving to our new home. Zoey was relaxed and calm until the weekend when it became very chaotic. While her limping didn't get any better, it also didn't get any worse. I called the vet and asked for additional meds. I had planned on taking her to a new vet on Monday closer to our new home, hoping he would be able to help us figure out what was going on. Right now I just needed to make her comfortable for a few days so she didn't aggravate her leg. Numerous people were in and out of the house that day and she found it difficult to be calm. She wanted our attention, but with so much to be done, we needed to be away from her and she needed to be out of the way. She was very nervous with all the commotion. It was not a restful weekend for her, but I would be off work all next week and we would figure out the issue and get it taken care of.

Bright and early Monday morning I called the vet office in our new town. They were very friendly as I explained the situation. They said the doctor had a few open times and he would like to examine her. I made an appointment for a little later that day. I called the vet that took the initial X-rays and asked the office to send Zoey's X-rays to the new vet. I asked them to make sure it was done as soon as possible so the new vet could take a look before our appointment that day.

I made the five-minute drive up the road with Zoey. Somehow I managed to get her in the car without any help, but I did ask for help taking her out of the car at the vet. The doctor was very nice and caring. He had taken a look at the X-rays and wanted to watch her walk. She was still limping, but her tail was straight out behind her wagging happily. She would do anything for me as long as she was with me.

We went into one of the exam rooms and talked a little bit. The doctor didn't know exactly what was going on. He said something didn't seem quite right and he thought we should see a specialist. He thought this was beyond his expertise and the best course of action was to have someone more versed assist with her care. He gave me the number to the specialist, asked me to let him know when her appointment was and they would send over the X-rays. Of course, I didn't make it home before I placed that call. Unfortunately, they were booked and we had to wait a couple of weeks. In that time, Zoey was babied even more if that was possible. We tried to limit her exercise as much as possible and just love on her. She was in heaven and couldn't have been happier. It was all about Zoey and nothing else mattered. From that time on, we dropped everything to just make her happy. We only unpacked a limited number of items so we could live in our home, but the rest of the time was devoted to her and only her.

Zoey was seen by the specialist on October 4th, 2018. He had viewed the previous X-rays and there was something that he did not like. However, the X-rays were not high enough up on her leg, so he wanted to take new X-rays of her leg closer to her shoulder. If the X-rays didn't show anything, he wanted to take an ultrasound and if that didn't reveal any problems, finally an

MRI. Of course, we would do whatever was necessary for her, so the procedure was scheduled for the morning of October 8th.

Tim dropped Zoey off in the morning for the procedure. The office was instructed to call me with updates and any findings. She would be the first appointment that morning, so she would be ready for me to pick her up on my way home from work. I wasn't worried. I knew it would be ok. Zoey would come home and we would continue living our lives in leisure out in the country.

I remember receiving the phone call later that morning from the specialist. He said there was not a good way to give me the news. In that moment, my heart stopped – the fear began to invade my body – I had to sit down. Not good news? How could it not be good news? She only hurt her leg and it could be fixed. He proceeded to tell me he didn't need to perform the ultrasound or MRI. The new X-rays showed him what he needed to know. Zoey's leg was fractured. They could not repair it. She had osteosarcoma, bone cancer, an aggressive cancer in her leg and it appeared to have already metastasized into her lung. He could not confirm the diagnosis, but he had seen this too many times before and he was certain it was cancer. They could do a biopsy to confirm the diagnosis before proceeding. What did I want to do? He recommended euthanasia or amputation of her leg.

What? What was happening? Zoey had cancer? How could this be? We took such good care of her. We gave her the best of everything. How could this happen? Why would anyone do this to her? She was the sweetest, most gentle being we have ever encountered. She didn't do anything wrong. This is not fair. How could anyone do this to her? Not our precious Zoey, not our baby girl. No! This could not be happening. We were supposed to live out our years together in our new home, out in the country where she could romp and play every day. No, No, No! Why? Why her? Why not some other? Why her? Please not my Zoey! Anything, but my Zoey. This was just too much to absorb. I had not expected any diagnosis like this and it was beyond my comprehension at the moment. I had to make a decision now? I can't do it. I love her so much, I can't lose her.

I can't lose her. I just can't. She's my baby girl. This is not possible. He's wrong. I began crying uncontrollably. The tears just streamed down my face. How could anyone take my Zoey from me? Didn't they know she was my world?

The doctor could tell I was not in any condition to make a decision now. He said to take the weekend, talk to my husband and come in on Monday. We would take as long as necessary to make certain whatever decision we would make would be the best for Zoey. He would wrap her leg so it was immobile and so no further damage could be done over the weekend. Our appointment was 9:00 a.m. on Monday.

I remember calling my husband and giving him the news. I remember he was as devastated as I was because she was also his girl. I remember our tears and I remember hanging up the phone with him. I walked around in a daze the rest of the day – crying and wondering why this was happening to her. I just wanted to get to her, hug her, hold her tight, and never let go.

Unfortunately, I wasn't able to bring Zoey home that night. She never did well while under anesthesia and when I went to pick her up that evening, she still seemed disoriented and not fully aware of her surroundings. She was still happy to see me and tried to get up and come to me, but she couldn't quite walk very well. I opted to leave her there for the night since it was a 24-hour emergency clinic so she could be monitored in case any issues came up. I asked if I could spend some time with her, so I laid in one of the exam rooms with her for several hours talking to her, stroking her face and telling her how much I loved her. I asked if I could spend the night, but they would not allow it. When they came to get her from the exam room, she whined and kept looking for me, looking to see if I was following behind, her eyes pleading for me to stay with her. I cried all the way home.

Tim and I went to pick her up the next afternoon. She looked so much more alert but was having problems maneuvering with the splint. She was still so happy to see us – tail wagging and whining to try and get to us. I fell to the floor and hugged her and kissed her. I just wanted to get her home.

I honestly don't remember much about that weekend. I remember picking her up and bringing her home. She was having a difficult time getting around with the splint and bandages. I remember we were in disbelief. I remember we cried. I remember we spent every moment with her. I remember she loved all the smothering attention.

Monday morning the specialist came into the exam room and introduced himself. I was sitting on the floor with Zoey. She was on her bed that we carried her in on. He showed us the X-rays and the cancer. We were still in shock and disbelief. We asked him what he would do especially since she was nine years old. He said he would do the amputation. He said animals are remarkable beings and have the ability to adjust to their situations better than humans. He said she would learn quickly how to get around on three legs. He has had several older animals adjust perfectly fine, but it was our decision. He told us to take as much time as we needed and he would check on us in a little bit. He said there is no rush – just make sure the decision you make is the right one for you.

The door closed and I immediately fell to my knees. I felt a pain in my heart like I had never felt before. A pain so deep it went all the way to my soul. I couldn't breathe, I couldn't walk, I couldn't sit, I couldn't do anything. I felt my world come crashing down. This was my Zoey. I didn't want to lose her, but was the amputation the best thing for her, or were we doing this for us? Could she do it? She was nine years old. It would be different if it were a back leg, but it's a front leg. She weighs 90 pounds. That is a lot to ask her to do. What were we supposed to do? She loved us and would do anything we asked her to do, but was it fair? Was it fair to her? Just because we didn't want to say goodbye was not a good enough reason. Zoey lived for us, but especially for me. She trusted us with her life.

This was going to be the most difficult decision we would have to make. How do we make that call? How do we take her life? How do we ask her to learn to do everything on three legs at nine years old? I had no answers, only questions and I couldn't answer any of them.

After about one and a half to two hours, we finally came to a decision. The doctor came back in and we told him we were going to give her a chance. We were going to give her a chance to live. She is a smart girl and we were going to give her the opportunity to try. We had to give her a chance. We just had to. We didn't want to wonder what if.

Just in case we had decided to move forward with the amputation, the doctor had scheduled time for Zoey that day. As they wheeled her away to surgery, she kept turning around looking at us, trying to find us, see where we were, see if we were following. My heart was breaking into a million little pieces. What if something went wrong? What if this is the last moment she sees me? She never liked the vet and now I was leaving her to undergo major surgery. I know she was terrified. I just had to believe it would all be fine, that she would see us again, I would see her again, and that this would not be our last memory of each other. I had to believe that or I may have collapsed at that very moment.

Later on that afternoon, the office called to let us know the surgery had gone well. Zoey was in recovery and waking up. As long as her vitals remained strong and she would eat, she would be able to come home tomorrow. I asked if I could come up and spend the night with her, but they thought it would cause her more stress and she needed to rest. I could call as many times as I wanted to check on her since there would be staff there all night. I felt better but didn't sleep that night. I just wanted to go get her and bring her home. I just wanted her to know I didn't leave her and that I would always be there for her.

We picked Zoey up at 2:00 p.m. the next day. It was agony waiting for her. How was she going to react? Was she going to be happy to see us? The door opened from the back and I heard her nails on the floor. As she approached the room she didn't see us at first, so I called her name. She finally saw us, but she was having a little trouble walking on the floor. The vet tech had a sling around her front to help her walk. She looked alert and was wagging her tail, but her reaction to us was a little muted. It was a shock to see her with her leg gone. She was shaved about 12 inches on the left side beginning at her neck to the middle of her back and about 18 inches from underneath her belly to the right side. The incision where they removed her leg was about 12 inches long and a small portion was showing from underneath the bandages. It was all red and swollen, but we didn't care. She was still our girl, our beautiful Zoey with her long, flowing fur. She was still beautiful to us and most importantly, she was still here. We could take her home.

Zoey was happy to be home, but this was going to be a learning experience for all of us. Tim helped her walk inside with the aid of the sling and we had her go into the living room. She laid on the floor in front of the fireplace and we both laid on the floor with her. We hugged and kissed on her and just loved her as much as she would let us. Her incision was not wrapped well around her shoulder-middle section and we were going to need to have it rewrapped. This meant another trip back to the specialist. She was not going to like that. We weren't sure how we were going to handle her situation, but we would try everything humanly possible to keep her with us. Our biggest obstacle right now was that Zoey could not get around without help and I did not have the strength to hold her up. Zoey was going to have to rely on Tim for help in going potty until she learned to do this on her own. This was not going to be easy, but we owed it to her.

That night we helped her up onto her bed, carried her bed into our bedroom and placed it where she would normally lay. You could tell she was a little out of it due to the pain meds, but we gave her the next dose and tried to go to sleep. At least she was home with us.

When I woke up the next morning, the first thing I did was check on her and make sure she was breathing. She looked at me, but it appeared as if she was looking right through me. Her eyes were glassy and it seemed like she didn't know where she was or who I was. Then I heard a noise and knew she was peeing. Something was not right. Zoey would never do anything like this. This wasn't normal and this wasn't Zoey. It was then those questions crept into my mind. What have we done? What did we do to her? Why did we do this to her? How selfish were we? Should we have just let her go?

I immediately called the vet and told them what was going on. They instructed me to reduce the amount of codeine she was taking. The dose may be too much for her and the primary concern was to keep her free of pain. We immediately cut the dosage in half and soon after, Zoey returned to being Zoey. She quickly learned to adjust to three legs and began to put her remaining front leg in the middle to balance herself. Within a week, she did not want our help any longer and refused to let us wrap the sling around her body. As best she could, she would run away from us when we approached her with the sling. She was going to do this on her own and she did. Zoey was truly amazing and nothing was going to slow her down. She was going to continue living and enjoying her life as long as possible. She was going to figure it out and find a way to do it differently if necessary. I truly was a lucky mom to have this girl in my life. She showed me how to fight and love with your whole being. I still can't believe I was chosen to be her mom.

We took her back in 12 days to have her sutures removed. The doctor said it looked good and was healing properly. Since it wasn't going to be wrapped any longer, he asked if I wanted a collar for her. He said she should not be allowed to lick it or scratch it. I told him she did not need a collar because all I had to do was tell her to leave it alone and she would. I don't think he believed me, but that is exactly what happened. She never touched her incision. That is how much she trusted me. She trusted me to make the best decisions for her and that is exactly what I always tried to do.

For the next six months we did everything possible with her and never left her alone for long. If she wanted to be outside, she was outside. I would wrap myself up in layers, cover up with many blankets and just sit with her – on the front porch, deck, driveway, in the grass – wherever she wanted to be. It didn't matter how cold, I was going to spend every moment with her. She would lay by me on the blanket keeping me warm. Sometimes we would share a pillow as we laid there for hours just looking at the world. We saw deer and turkey while we watched the world go by. She was so excited to see them and I was so excited for her.

No matter where we were or what we were doing, we always included her and found a way to make certain she was with us. Whether we were on the deck or sitting outside in the grass, she was always right next to me with her head on my lap. I enjoyed every moment of this time with her. I was just a girl with her dog. Life was as good as it could be given the circumstances, but most importantly, I still had my girl. I was going to make certain she was happy, comfortable and loved. This was my only goal, my only concern, nothing else mattered now.

We put area rugs down all over the house to help Zoey get around. We turned the living room into Zoey's area and put down numerous blankets, beds, pillows, whatever was necessary to keep her comfortable. We even began to sleep on the floor next to her; one of us on the floor next to her and one of us on the couch. I promised her when I brought her home I would never let her sleep alone and I intended to honor that promise. We would go above and beyond for her. We owed this to her.

However, this time did not come without its problems. It seemed like every week brought a new one. First, we fought through Zoey not wanting to eat. We were told she might be depressed after the amputation and would not be interested in food. Again, those horrible questions began to surface. What do we do? What have we done? I even tried hand feeding her, but she did not want anything to do with food. I pleaded with her, I begged her, I cried and tried to reason with her, but she would not eat. Then one Sunday my nephew and his wife came to visit Zoey. She was so happy to see Brad and hopped out to greet him. He had watched her for us so many times and loved her too. When he saw her, he had to fight back the tears. He did not know about the amputation and it was quite a lot to take in at one time. He leaned down to her, buried his face in her fur and just held onto her.

Later that evening, they watched as I tried to get her to eat from my hand, but she did not want anything to do with it. Brad got up from his chair, sat on the floor next to her, grabbed some of her food in his hand and tried to coax Zoey into eating. At that moment, Zoey relented and began eating from his hand. He grabbed some more of her food and she ate more. Zoey was finally eating! Brad always had a special bond with dogs throughout his life. Apparently, Zoey was waiting for him.

Next, we battled through Horner's disease. Zoey had lost her balance going to the bathroom and fell in the yard. The next day her right eye began to sag, and the third eyelid began to cover her eye. We traveled to numerous doctors looking for answers and help. We finally found another specialist that diagnosed her correctly. He said the disease could be brought on by high stress or a fall. We had both of those covered. He said her eye may or may not return to normal, but it was not painful and she still had the ability to see. I just couldn't understand why this was happening to her. Why did she have to go through all of this? Hasn't she been through enough? Why would someone do this to her? The sweetest, most gentle soul did not deserve this. This was not fair. How much more was she expected to endure?

Our next dilemma was when she decided to stop drinking water. I took her to the vet twice for subcutaneous fluids. I began giving her ice cubes just to get some fluids into her. This was our ritual morning, noon, and night. I was terrified. What was going on? Why was she doing this? She had to drink water. She could not survive without water. I would do anything. Please just drink for me. Again, I pleaded and begged her to drink. Then one day she just started drinking again. I began to wonder what was next. What is the next issue to come up? It wouldn't be long and I would have my answer.

The month of December finally rolled around and Zoey's nose began to drain. It wasn't much at first, but more than normal and I began to worry. Zoey and I were so in tune with each other, I just knew when something wasn't right. Once again, we were at the vet's office.

They took some blood and ran a complete health scan. All the tests came back normal considering her situation. Still, I knew something wasn't right and so we started her on amoxicillin and Benadryl. This seemed to work, but only for a short time.

Eventually, the draining of her nose started to get worse and worse and she began to develop a cough. We stopped the Benadryl and began giving her Zyrtec since it lasted longer along with the amoxicillin. We had to increase the dose of Zyrtec every couple of weeks as the draining and coughing got worse. I called every vet and specialist in the area looking for answers, looking for someone to help me figure this out. I wasn't giving up on her, I would never give up on her, but it seemed I couldn't find anyone willing to delve deeper to find out what was going on. I would have paid any amount of money. It didn't matter. I had to help her. Why wouldn't anyone help me? Don't they understand how much she means to me? She is my world; she is my heart. Please someone help me! I had to do everything humanly possible to help my girl. I did not want to look back and wonder if there was something more I could do. I had to exhaust every option. I wouldn't be able to live with myself if there was something more I could do.

In February 2019, I was able to get Zoey an appointment with a well-renowned college veterinary school specializing in cancer. I finally had someone willing to help me and now we would find answers. They did an examination and did not note anything abnormal. Given Zoey's condition, the vet thought she was adjusting well. They recommended a CT scan of the entire body. If there was anything abnormal noted on the scan, we could discuss a course of action. Of course, I opted to go forward with the CT scan. They would send the scan to a radiologist who would interpret it and the doctor would call me with the results. Finally – some answers.

The doctor called at 6:00 p.m. two days later. I didn't think the results could be any worse than when I found out she had cancer. Well, I was wrong. The CT scan revealed Zoey had three masses on her lung and had also developed a brain tumor.

What? Why? Why is this happening to her? My beautiful girl. Hasn't she been through enough? Why? She did nothing wrong. All she did was love us. Was that wrong? This can't be happening again. The realization finally set in. No matter what we do, we were going to lose her. We were going to lose Zoey. I was going to lose my heart and soul and there was nothing more I could do.

I hung up the phone and walked over to the couch where Tim was sitting. I looked at him and the tears began to fall. I couldn't even get the words out to tell him. My world had truly crashed around me. My world had fallen apart.

We made the decision to keep Zoey as comfortable and happy as possible for any time she had remaining with us. We would love her to the end and one day have to make that horrible decision to let her go. I knew it was going to have to be my decision and I didn't know if I could do it, but I remembered that promise I made to her so long ago. I would not let her suffer.

Throughout the entire ordeal, Zoey was so strong. She never whined. She never showed any signs of pain. Any time she was with us, she was happy. She devoted her life to being with us. She made coming home the best part of each day. To see her greet me each evening was truly amazing. She would hop like a bunny on those three legs as fast as she could to get to me. I would sit down by her and let her lick my face over and over. She would whine in excitement to see me. It was the best part of her day. It was the best part of my day. Her mom was home.

Each day that passed from that October day was a blessing. I tried to remember that, but each day that she was with us, I just wanted to have another and another. Each day she was with us was going to make it harder and harder to let her go.

By March, her fur had almost completely grown back in and her eye had turned to normal. She was still crossing her front paw as if she still had both of them. She would just put her remaining paw in the middle and tilt it sideways. If it was possible, she was even more precious to us. Zoey was always beautiful, but now she was returning to her princess status.

It was now April and Zoey's appetite had started to decrease. She was not eating twice a day any longer and she would not eat from her bowl. I was able to get her to eat by hand feeding her, but I think she was only doing it as a courtesy to me. She was still happy, but it was getting more difficult for her to move around without coughing. I knew the time was coming. I knew I was going to have to make that decision, that final act of love. I still didn't know if I could do it. I still was holding on to hope, any hope that this was just a dream or that somehow a miracle would occur. I just couldn't give up. I wasn't going to give up on her. She brought so much joy to our lives, so much happiness. This couldn't be the end.

The nights began to be bad for her. She couldn't get comfortable and was always hot. The coughing always seemed to be the worst at night and none of us were getting any sleep. She would want to be outside where it was colder and where her cough seemed to subside a little. That was the only place now where she seemed to be happy, so we made the decision to start sleeping in the garage with the door up. We put dog beds together with several blankets and sleeping bags and began to sleep outside every night in the garage. Zoey would be right next to us on her bed. Her coughing did not seem to be as bad and all of us were able to get some sleep. We would huddle together, the three of us, side by side for warmth. We would fall asleep looking up at the stars and the sounds of nature that come out at night. I would wish upon a star every night asking for Zoey to be better, for Zoey to be healed, for this stupid cancer to go away, but knowing in my heart I wasn't going to get the answer I wanted, knowing in my heart that time was approaching and our time together was coming to an end. It was the three of us – our little family – Tim, Zoey, and me. We would do anything to keep her comfortable and happy for as long as we could. We would do anything or give anything to keep her here with us.

One morning we were in the garage and Zoey had a coughing spell. I laid down next to her until it passed, but there was something different I had not seen before. There was something red on the floor that was not there before she began coughing. I touched it between my fingers and began to cry. Zoey had coughed up blood for the first time. My heart broke into a million pieces again. I was crushed and sat there in disbelief. I knew the time was coming, but I was hoping for a miracle, hoping it wouldn't progress, hoping I wouldn't have to make that call. Each additional day she stayed with us, I kept hoping and wishing and praying and begging for another and another. I had begun to talk myself into believing maybe she would be with me for another day, week, another month, another year. But at that moment, I knew. It all came crashing down on me. The pain, the heartbreak, the agony of never seeing her again, touching her again. In my head, I was screaming. *This can't be happening; this can't be it. I don't have the strength to do this. I can't make that decision.* But I knew she was counting on me, I knew she trusted me and I knew I was going to have to say goodbye.

Zoey took her last breath on April 16th, 2019. The vet arrived at our home around 11:30 a.m. The rest is somewhat of a blur. She knocked on the door and Zoey hopped to the door, barking with her loud, deep bark. At that moment, I began to question our decision. Are we doing the right thing? Is this the right time? She's still happy, wagging her tail, protecting us. How could we do this to her? It's not her time. But the coughing got the best of her and I knew we were making the right decision as difficult as it was.

We had to make her lay down. Tim laid on the floor with her, touching her long, soft fur, telling her it would be ok. He stayed with her as I talked to the vet. I don't remember what was said. I was just looking at Zoey and concentrating on her, trying to remember every last spot, shape, mark, just everything about her, everything. Once she calmed down, we had her come back into the living room onto the blankets where we had laid with her for the past six months day and night – holding her, loving her, and never wanting to let her go. We held her in our arms, my head as close to hers as I could possibly get. With tears streaming down our faces, Tim ran his hands across her entire body and I stroked her head over and over. We were doing everything possible to remember every little thing about her. From the brown fur around her mouth, to the black and white whiskers, to the expressive brown circles above her eyes, her long, beautiful eyelashes, the long, soft, flowing fur that covered her entire body, to the white at the tip of her tail. We didn't want to forget anything about her.

I cupped her sweet face in both my hands and told her how much I loved her. I told her it would be ok and that grandpa was waiting for her. As she slowly began to close her eyes and drift off to sleep, her head began to drop and I held it in my hands, nose to nose. I promised her the day I brought her home, I would be the last face she ever saw and my voice would be the last sound she ever heard. I promised her I would never let her suffer. As difficult as it was, I kept those promises. I owed it to her after the tremendous joy she had brought to my life. She slowly closed her eyes one last time and her gorgeous head got heavier and heavier. I kissed her and at that moment I knew she was gone. Our precious baby, our joy had left this world. The tears rolled down my face and Tim and I cried uncontrollably. We both held her close, not wanting to let her go. Not wanting this to be the final time we saw her, touched her, kissed her, and hugged her. I remember thinking, *this isn't real. It's just a dream. She's going to wake up. She didn't just leave us. How could this be happening? She was so sweet, so perfect. She didn't deserve this fate. How could anyone do this to her? It's not fair. We were supposed to have more time together. This was to be the beginning of spending more time together, not the end.* But that is not how it turned out.

We held on to Zoey trying to remember everything about her – her soft, wavy fur, her beautiful long nose, the shape of her head and body, everything. It wouldn't be enough to last a lifetime, but we didn't have a choice. I don't know how much time had passed, but we wrapped Zoey in a blanket and carried her out to the car. I remember thinking she wouldn't want this blanket on her as she was always hot. We placed her in the back and I held her face in my hands one last time. I placed my head on her head and told her again how much I loved her. I kissed her over and over knowing this would be the last time I would be able to touch her, feel her, see her. As the vet closed the door, I wanted to run and open it, hold her in my arms again, and take her back. Was this really happening? This can't be real. It has to be a bad dream, but I knew better. The car pulled away and Tim and I dropped to our knees. It took every ounce of strength to not run after the car and take one last glimpse, just one last kiss, one last touch. She was our life for the last nine and a half years and our lives were forever changed by the love of this beautiful, precious soul. She was intertwined with our hearts. How do we go on without her? I didn't have an answer and I still don't. Her death has brought me to my knees with grieving and rocked me to the core of my very being. The hurt and pain are immense and seem insurmountable. I don't think I'll ever be able to let her go. I don't think I'll truly ever be able to say goodbye.

As I finish writing this, it has only been three months since we said goodbye to our little girl and tears are streaming down my cheeks. I've cried every day since and will cry every day for a long time, maybe forever. Nothing feels the same anymore, home doesn't feel like home and life doesn't seem like life without her in it. Zoey wasn't just a pet or just a dog or even just a member of the family. Zoey was our sweet, beautiful, perfect, and precious princess. She was our baby, our child, our daughter, our heart, and our world. She was the light of our lives – she was our heart dog. She was always there, always with us, and always by our side. Our constant companion day and night. We loved her as much as she loved us. She is forever etched in our minds, heart, and soul. There will never be another like her. There will never be another her.

We were the lucky ones, however – lucky to be her parents, lucky to have her in our lives, and lucky to be able to love her with our entire being. As much as it hurts, I wouldn't change any of it. I was able to experience a love with her like no other. A love that transcends this world, a love I will carry with me until my last breath.

Zoey. Her name means life. She was my life…she could not have had a better name. It fit her perfectly. I will hold her in my heart forever. It's not enough, but it will have to be. It's all I have until hopefully we meet again.

Zoey

What I Learned from Twister
By Anne Golembeski

As I observe my beautiful little girl Twister in the last days of her life, I have to find meaning in her being. She was never meant to be a therapy dog. Her obsessive spinning and licking ensured that. She was never meant to be a hunting dog. Her over-the-top anxiety prevented that. Her incontinence meant she wasn't wanted by someone. She was, however, wanted by me. I remember the day she came to live with us so clearly. I knelt down in a scrum of dogs to see if I had a connection with any of them. Between the legs and shoulders of bigger Brittanys emerged a small face with bright eyes and a lolling tongue. "Me! Pick me!" I swear I distinctly heard her say. "I'm the one!" And so she was.

This squirming, skinny, flying, obsessive little girl joined our lives.

My husband was not convinced that he could love this strange little dog. She didn't know that, nor did she care. She followed him around the house as he worked and carefully observed everything he did. Supervisor Twister became the quality-control expert. She tilted her head and stared intently at any work being done as if trying hard to comprehend. Her attention was only broken to spin occasionally when my husband let loose with cuss words. One day he called her "Poppa's girl." I had lost my dog, and it felt good.

She was chosen to fill an empty spot in our home left by the passing of my beloved and brilliant Massimo. Massimo's death left our other Brittany, Val, terribly lonely and inconsolably lost. Saving a life and providing him companionship seemed natural. We had no idea how much she would be needed until Val lost his eyesight just a year later. She became his eyes, his support, his companion. She was patient and alert with him always. But Val, too, was destined to leave this world and after a brief illness, he was gone, and our home and hearts were empty.

Liam joined our family, adopted from the same place Twister came from. Twister became the trouble-making elder sister to Liam's more serious personality. Every morning and every evening, Twister and Liam had loud and energetic mock fights covering the house and yard. Their growling was ferocious and their enjoyment uncontainable. As the sun sank and cooler evening temperatures arrived, I smiled at the sound of their play in the backyard.

While Liam was aloof with our neighbor's two standard poodles, Twister became obsessed with them. Hearing their barks from across the street caused her to leap with joy. Shared evenings were filled with Twist taunting and racing with Stan and Murph, up and down the stairs and across the cool grass. She would cry out in pretend fear when they ganged up on her and then throw herself at them when they backed away. Exhausted and covered in drool, she would smile hugely and with great satisfaction.

Occasionally her incontinence would pop up, and she would wake us up with her anxious spinning. She would look fearfully for the punishment to come. Of course, it never came. Diapers came and more medications until it was again controlled, and she could sleep undisturbed.

Twist became my wardrobe consultant. She would perch on a small ottoman in the closet and pronounce *yea* or *nay* on my choice of blouses. I tried to tell her that there were no princess gowns hanging on my racks, just jeans and shirts but she never stopped looking for them. Twist would stare at me with deep brown eyes trying telepathically to get me to buy something worthy of a princess. I tried to convince her she was the only princess in the house.

Twist intently observed me drying my hair, clearly horrified anyone would wash their hair much less put that roaring monster of a dryer near it. In an effort to dim the horror, she would wipe her face on my husband's damp towel hanging nearby. That was our secret.

She welcomed overnight doggie visitors who were en route to new lives with an open heart or at least unquenchable curiosity. Twist was baffled when Mocha wrinkled her lips at her. She played endlessly with Titan. She followed Ozzie around clearly impressed that doghood came in such a small package. She fell head over heels in love with Kona the dachshund whose stay was as short as his legs.

Bullwinkle arrived a few days before Thanksgiving one year. He was a refugee from the Manhattan ACC. Twister was not amused. Bullie was not amused either. Like most rescues, it took a year for him to decompress. He tried to play with Twist, but his hulking size was too much for her, and she snarled at him. He backed away. Bullie stared longingly at Liam and Twist when they played. He would insert himself between the two, and Twist would lecture him on his manners. Slowly, Bullie learned to be gentle, and Twist quit lecturing. And one day, they played. Bullie may not have played in years, if ever in his life. Twist gave him the gift of play and joy.

Now my little girl is very sick. Her liver and her kidneys are failing her. Her favorite pastime in the world, eating, is lost to her. Every day taking her medications is difficult and frustrating. She sleeps a lot. She gets nauseous a lot. She doesn't have the energy she had a few short months ago and sometimes she stumbles. One day she leapt on her ottoman in the closet and fell off the other side. She wants to eat but can't eat. Still, her megawatt smile shines. Her eyes are bright. She snuggles close at night between my husband and me and I feel her beating heart against my stomach.

Twister did not have big adventures. We took her once to an American Brittany Rescue picnic in Colorado, but I had intended to take her back to Silver City where she was initially dumped in a kill shelter. I had intended to take her to play in the ocean. I had intended to show her our land in Wyoming. Still, Twist doesn't care. Her life was not meant to be large. It was meant to be meaningful.

Twist accepts all without judgment, despite her anxiety. She gave comfort to Val. She was Liam's lighter side. She taught Bullie to play. She never let the bigger, faster, stronger dogs intimidate her. She lives every day of her small life to the fullest. Twist's life has meaning because she didn't wait for something to give it meaning; she lives her life with meaning. That's what I learned from Twister. We all make our own meaning, both large and small.

Twister

He Wrote His Name on My Heart
By Anne Golembeski

Within the space of a few days, several amazing gifts and expressions of love arrived at my home. That's because, within the space of a few months, I lost my happy little dancer, Twister, and then her playmate, Bullwinkle.

We knew Twist was going to be leaving us and it was carefully arranged so that we could be there to help her cross the Bridge. It hurt like hell and our house felt empty because, despite her small size, Twist was a huge personality.

We did not have that luxury with Bullwinkle. He left as unexpectedly as he arrived. I saw his face on Beth Gillian's Facebook page and was transfixed. Something in his eyes and the angle of his ears captured me. One day he was on death row at the Manhattan ACC a thousand miles away, and the next, he was my dog. Bullwinkle was fascinating on many levels. He was a mystery to me. Where did he live? What was his life like? What had he seen, and who had loved him? What was his last walk to the ACC like? His picture tells the story of a dog who was terrified.

He was physically beautiful. I can feel his muscles and the hard smoothness of his coat. I wasn't used to that, having had Brittanys for so many years. His wrinkles were like another world to me. How could those silly little ears express so much emotion? His coat was golden brown tipped with black. It shimmered. And then the remarkable gray of his muzzle and eyebrows just took my breath away. Finally, a dashing strip of white on his chest completed his handsomeness. Unlike Liam, his eyes were so deep and dark that trying to read what he was thinking was impossible, but those ears and that whip-like tail told me everything I needed to know.

He was gentle. I woke up his first morning here to his giant head in my face and his tail whump, whump, whumping the wall next to my bed. Bullie's kisses were so soft. I was afraid he might hurt Twist or Liam because he was so much bigger, but when Twist put him in his place, he just rolled on his back and grinned while she harassed him. I can see him coming around the corner of the house, his eyes inscrutable until he saw me, then his ears moved, and his tail swung, and he broke into a lumbering lope.

He was the first truly good thing I ever did in my life. I looked at his picture, and I said, "I can cry, or I can try." My "trying" was pretty weak. I knew he would never be adopted by someone in New Mexico. Then the miracle that was Bullie happened. Those who tried harder than me arrived out of the blue. Beth demanded he be rescued and adopted by me. Cecelia Blake descended like a guardian angel to beg, bribe, and beat strangers into bringing Bullwinkle home.

Cecelia, Beth, Donna, Karen K., Karen L., Susan F., and Ladonna M. did something that takes my breath away to this day. They brought Bullie all the way from New York to New Mexico. No one in my entire life had ever done anything like that for me. They thought they were doing it for Bullie, but they really did it for me. They made me believe in something I had not believed in for a long, long time. Miracles and the goodness of humans. Sometimes I would be lost in thought just staring at Bullie and imagining all he had seen and all those he had touched and how somehow, like a falling star, he was here in my home. A miracle. A real-life miracle.

Then he was gone. Just as I was truly beginning to know who Bullwinkle was, he left. He was fine, and then he wasn't. That quick. As quickly as I found out we were his new family, we found out he was leaving. I wasn't there to tell him one more time how much I loved him. I didn't get to kiss his blocky head or stroke his strong body. I didn't get to touch his funny little ears. I didn't get to tell him to look for Twister, or Massimo, or Val, or Beau, or Barney. I'm sorry, Therese, Stacey F, Linda C., Jennifer D, Beth G, Cecelia B, Donna W, Karen K, Karen L, Susan F, Ladonna M, and everyone who loved Bullie. I'm sorry I couldn't save him after all.

I can't even begin to know how to let go of this. Then the cards with healing well-wishes arrived. One of my lovely friends sent me a Rainbow Bridge bracelet that I can wear along with Twister's so they are together again. Other friends sent me a hurricane lantern with Bullie's picture. It meant so much. Bullie and Twist can now light my evenings with their beautiful faces glowing softly together. What a wonderful gift from wonderful people. People I don't even know, who followed Bullie's story with so much hope, made it possible to donate to Connect-a-Pet New England, Mended Hearts Rescue – Friends of Gladys, and Jethro's Animal Sanctuary. That makes my heart so filled with gratitude. Then came the wind chimes giving my Bullie a voice again. The words on it say:

I wrote your name in the sky, but the wind blew it away.
I wrote your name in the sand, but the waves washed it away.
I wrote your name in my heart, and forever it will stay.

Yes. That's exactly right. Bullwinkle's name will stay in my heart forever, even though the wind blew him away. Now Twist and Bullie dance in the wind together. Instead of waking at night to his soft snoring, I wake to the tones of him and Twist playing among the stars. Your kindness and generosity are miracles too. They overwhelm me, heal me, humble me. We don't deserve all this.

Thank you, generous friends. Thank you to everyone who followed Bullwinkle's journey and loved him as much as I do. Thank you for recognizing that a dog like Bullie doesn't just pass away without leaving a huge hole in everyone's heart.

Bullie

Dexter
By Bonnie Lee

It was in December the first time I laid eyes on him, curled up next to his brothers and sisters in a cardboard box. It was raining, and we were at the dollar store getting Christmas decorations. There were a couple of kids out front holding a box with puppies in it. Of course, I had to look, and there he was. I knew at that moment we were meant to be together. He was the only red one; the others were blue. I asked my fiancé, Mark, if I could have him. He said *no, it wasn't a good time*, we had just moved, and life was just kind of hectic at the time. We walked to the truck, and he started to drive off. He looked over at me and saw the disappointment on my face. Then he turned the truck around, stopped, and told me to go get one. Best $20 I have ever spent in my life. He fit in the palms of my hands. He was just a little ball of fur. He stole my heart from the beginning. I named him Dexter, and it suited him well. From that day on, we were together 24/7. My youngest child had just left home, and Dexter filled a void that was there. I had someone that needed me, and I needed him.

I watched him grow into a beautiful boy. I nursed him through a bought of parvo when he was about one. Dexter's eyes were a little droopy and one slightly crossed, but that didn't matter. To me, he was perfect. When he was about six months old, he and his friend (a pitty), who belonged to a neighbor, were chasing the neighbor's horse (it was their favorite pastime). That day the horse didn't want to be chased, and he kicked the pit. He flew, and when he hit the ground, he was dead. My neighbor heard the ruckus and ran out in time to see my boy flying through the air. My neighbor yelled my name and said, *Dexter!* – that's all I needed to hear. The sound of his voice told me something was wrong. I ran out, looking where he was walking, and saw my boy crumpled on the ground. My heart was pounding. I ran as fast as I could to him. I dropped to my knees next to him and picked him up. He opened his eyes and licked the tears off my face. I looked at him, and I couldn't believe my boy was alright. The only thing that happened was his eyes were no longer crossed. The kick did nothing to my hard-headed boy except uncross his eyes.

We moved when Dexter was about one and a half years old. After growing up with two acres to run and play in, I'm sure the yard we had at the new place probably seemed pretty cramped to him. But we were by a river, and we often went to play by it. Dexter did not like water. He would not go in no matter how hard we tried to get him to. But he loved tennis balls and squeaky toys. His love for tennis balls outweighed his hate for water. If I threw a ball in the river, he would go in, reluctantly, to get his ball and right back to dry land. He was so funny, so unique, so handsome. He went everywhere with us.

My boy was a free spirit and loved to run around. I kept finding him gone out of the yard. Sometimes he would be sitting outside our yard waiting to be let back in. Sometimes we had to go look for him. Those times I would almost have a panic attack if he wasn't found right away. I know how cruel people can be, and I didn't want my boy to know anything but love. I really didn't think Dex was jumping the fence; it was six feet. One day, Dex was outside, and I was inside. I heard a bark I had never heard before from him. I ran out, and he was hanging by his collar on the fence, my neighbor Bob was there as fast as I was, and he helped get my boy free. He told me he wasn't jumping the fence; he was climbing it as a human would. Well, I don't think he climbed it again after that day. He found another way to get out.

In the new place, the gate had a latch mechanism. One day I went outside, and the gate was wide open with Dex gone. I could usually find him across the street from us. There was a girl dog that Dex had a crush on. Anytime he would see her, he would run, get his ball, and bounce and catch it while looking at her. When she passed by or went inside, he would drop his ball and lay down. I have never seen a dog show off as he did.

I had found the gate open on several occasions and more frequently as time went by. Then one day, Bob came by to tell me he had solved the mystery of who was letting my boy out. He was letting himself out. Bob watched him as he lifted the latch with his nose and pushed the gate open. So, we started putting a lock on it. My boy never ceased to amaze me. He was my pride and joy.

He loved the grandkids and welcomed each new baby. He saw them as someone new to throw his ball. Before they could sit up, Dexter was dropping his ball in their lap, trying to teach them to throw as soon as possible. He was funny and determined.

He was very protective of us. We would walk to the store and he would stand by the gate and watch us, he would be at the same spot when we came back, waiting for us. I still look for him whenever I come back from a walk. My heart drops when I don't see him, my vision blurs and my throat burns with that lump that is all too familiar.

Dexter had a sense of humor like no dog I've ever known. There was a chain link fence between our house and our neighbor, Bob. I think Dex was Bob's therapist. He would sit outside by the fence and talk to Dex for hours. Once in a while, Dex would bark, and Bob would give him a piece of beef jerky. Dex had a game he played. Whenever Bob was coming or going, Dexter would hide behind a rose bush and jump out and bark as Bob walked past. Bob would jump, startled. "Damn it, Dexter, you got me again," Bob would chuckle. I love my boy so much and miss him terribly.

When I say Dexter loved to play fetch, I mean he loved to play fetch. He never tired of it. We tried to outlast him but could never do it. At times he was just a little too demanding of someone to play with him. We would be doing yard work, I would be raking, and Dex would drop his ball right where I was raking because he knew I would pick it up and toss it out of my way. He would drop it in front of Mark mowing the lawn. He would pick it up and throw it. But after the fifth or sixth time, he would tell Dexter *no more* and hide the ball. You couldn't hide his ball from him, however. He found it no matter where Mark hid it. Trash can, in the car, on the roof, even buried it once – my boy found it every time. Dexter was a great companion to have. He filled my life with so much joy.

We moved one last time when Dexter was seven years old. By this time, I had four other fur babies; two of them were Dexter's daughters, Della and Stella.

Even though I relive this every day, it doesn't make it any easier to write. We lived here for three years when my stepdaughter, from a previous marriage, called needing a place to stay. She just got out of jail and was on a monitoring program. Hindsight is 20/20. I wish I would have said no, but I didn't. She had been here a few weeks when a probation officer came knocking on my door. As much as I do not want to include him in this, I must. My fur babies and I were relaxing in my room watching TV; the door was shut. When they all stood up and started barking, well, that told me someone was at the gate. People normally do not come into my yard. I have 'beware of dog' signs posted. I get up, and of course, I'm almost run over by five dogs wanting to get to the door before me, and they did. When I walked into the living room, I saw someone holding the doggie door closed. That didn't sit well with my dogs, so it was hard to get them back. I asked who it was, and as I did, I saw a laser light like on a laser pen. I heard him say *probation*, and as he did, a thought flashed through my mind, *he's going to shoot my dogs.* I told him to give me a minute to secure them. I put them back in my room and went to let the officers in. He was there, of course, to see my stepdaughter, who wasn't home. I was talking to one of them while the other was searching her room. He asked what kind of dogs I have; I told him Dex was a Queensland. I knew he would be back, and because of the danger that flashed through my mind, I asked him if he would call before he came out. I asked him at least three times because I wanted to ensure my dogs would be safe. He assured me he would every time. He even said, "I have two cattle dogs. I would hate if something happened to them." They eventually left, and I felt I had nothing to fear regarding my dogs. I trusted him, he said he would call, and I believed him. I grew up in the 70s when law enforcement officers were there to help you. I was raised believing the police were our friends.

July 31st, 2014, at about 7:30 p.m., Mark, myself, and my stepdaughter were in the living room watching TV, we had just finished eating and we were settling down to watch a movie. Dexter could hear the gate across the street opening and he would run outside and bark. That evening he ran outside barking and all the other dogs followed. But I knew his barks. I knew if his bark meant someone was walking by or at the people across the street or another dog. They were all different, and this bark was someone was in his yard. I'm not a people person, I don't care to have people at my house. The only people that do come over are my children and grandchildren Dex did not bark at them. Not too many people would come into my yard anyway. There was only one person that would come by to see Mark. He'd walk in the yard and Dex would corral him in a corner, the poor guy would just stand there with his hands up telling Dex, *it's ok boy.* When Dexter would see me walk in the yard, he would come stand in front of me until the guy got out of the yard.

I said to Mark, "Someone is in the yard!" We got up at the same time. As he was stepping out the door, me one step behind him, I hear four-gun shots – pow, pow, pow, pow – I jumped out the door, turned, and saw my boy laying on the sidewalk, three and a half feet away from the opened gate; his back legs twitched twice then he was still.

I couldn't believe what I was seeing. It took a minute for it to register in my brain what just happened. I could hear Mark yelling. "You shot my dog!" It sounded like he was a million miles away. Then I heard a wailing, a heart-wrenching scream. As I ran to my boy, I realized that scream was coming from me. It felt like it took forever to reach him. When I did, I stopped and sat down by his side, I gently put his head on my lap, and I told him what a good boy he was; I told him how much I loved him and that he didn't deserve to die this way. I told him how sorry I was that I had failed him. I didn't keep him safe. But my boy was already gone. I couldn't see or hear anyone. I didn't want to, really. The only thing on my mind was my Dexter. There was a knot in my stomach, and it was getting hard to breathe. I don't know how long I sat there with my face in my boy's fur. When I finally looked up, I was looking into the eyes of the man that had just murdered my soul animal. I wanted to stand up and hit him, rip his face off, to do to him what he had just done to my boy. I wanted to claw his eyes out. I wanted to reach into his chest and rip his heart out and throw it on the ground next to mine. But all I could do was ask *why*. I must have asked him a million times. "Why? Why did you shoot him? You told me you would call...you told me you would call!" I hear him say in an emotionless voice, "I was under no obligation to call you ma'am." Those words just dumbfounded me. I didn't know what to do, what to say. I sat there with my boy's head in my lap crying.

At some point, I remember seeing my stepdaughter and her saying, "I'm sorry, momma." Before long, more police cars were there. Animal control came, I glared at him, daring him to touch my boy. One of the police officers told me he was there to confirm that Dex was dead. I thought, *are these people really that stupid*? I turned to look for Mark and I saw him sitting, facing the side of the house with his hands behind his back handcuffed. I was so angry. These people just came into my yard and shot and killed my dog for no reason. "What the hell, why is he handcuffed?" The reason I was told it was for the officer's safety. Well, they handcuffed the wrong person. If anyone, I would be the one they needed to fear. More police came to do an "investigation." Which, as far as I could tell, consisted of them standing in my yard chatting. By this time, I was inside trying to ward off an asthma attack. I must have been worse than I thought, as a policeman kept asking me if I wanted an ambulance. I would have died right there before I left and trusted them with my boy's body.

When they finally left, and I had to make the decision of what I was going to do with my boy, I didn't want to take him anywhere. I didn't want to put him in the ground. I wanted him to stay with me. I knew I would never see him again. I just couldn't bring myself to take him anywhere. I was finally talked into letting him go, literally. But I told my boy I would make that son of a bitch pay for what he did. My daughter took him to the ER vet to be cremated. I didn't know what to do; I was so angry and hurt. I remember just being so angry as I made a sign that was probably fifteen feet long and four feet tall. I got my paint out, and I wrote:

Probation Officer Carlos, you lied. You said you would call me, instead, you came and shot and killed my best friend. *Why?*

I didn't want Mark to wash off the blood where Dexter lay. I just felt that was all I had left of him and if it was gone, it would be too final. The next six months consisted of tears and nightmares. The sound of the gunshots is forever in my mind. With all that going on, I didn't even think about my other babies. I remember seeing them run past me into the house when I was running out. I went and laid down sometime after midnight. That was the first I had seen the others. They were all on my bed huddled together; I hugged and kissed each one, while the bigger ones went to their beds, except Della, she stayed on my pillow and would not move, she was petrified. I let her stay there. I don't think she laid down once. Della was very close to her dad, Dexter. I couldn't imagine the trauma she was experiencing. I sat next to her and gave her a hug and just reassured her she was alright. She didn't want to eat and that was *not* like Della. Finally, she got up to go outside reluctantly. When she came in I noticed she was limping. I went to her and started running my fingers over her. I didn't feel anything and there was no blood. I thought, *she couldn't have been shot too.* I called her up on to me and when she stood up on her hind legs, I saw it. Center mast in her chest, there was a bullet hole. I think my heart stopped beating for a second or two. The knot in my throat doubled in size, it was so hard to breathe. I was about to panic – I didn't want her walking – I didn't know if the bullet exited or if it was still in there. Is it close to her heart? If she moves, will it kill her? Why wasn't there blood? Oh, my poor girl, I'm so sorry you were in pain all night. Please don't let me fail her like I did her dad.

Our regular vet was closed so I took her to a different office and I told them what happened. They took X-rays to see where the bullet lodged. She was one of the luckiest dogs in the world that day. They explained that the bullet didn't go straight in. They said it traveled down and lodged closer to her front leg. That made perfect sense. Whenever Dex was outside, Della was always right by his side. If he was running, she was next to him jumping up on him trying to get his attention. I'm sure that's when she was shot. The vet doctor said to just leave the bullet in her. But a follow-up with our own vet a few days later determined Della had to have surgery as it was getting infected around the bullet. Seeing her before she went under, I prayed it wouldn't be the last time I saw her alive. The surgery took longer than expected, but she came through. It seemed like I was holding my breath the entire time and finally I could breathe again.

She had drain tubes put in and the doctor said she had to go deeper than she thought, there was so much infection and hair tangled in there. She wanted to be sure she got it all. Della had to keep the drain tubes in for close to seven weeks. Even in as much pain as she was, when they were bringing her to me, she heard my voice and started jogging to me – butt wiggling out of control. So was mine. I was just as happy to see her. They gave me the bullet they dug out of her. I don't remember the caliber but it was a hollow point. I thought they were outlawed – well they should be. Della's recovery was slow. Out of all of them, she grieved for Dex the most. She would go outside and lay in the spot her daddy was laying when he died. She would lay there for hours. I helped her as best I could, my grief being so overwhelming.

I won't go into all the legal parts of this, but my sign stayed up on my house and it was very effective. I met people from across town that had heard about my sign.

We had our boy cremated and now he sits in the hall next to my bedroom door, with his bowl, collar, and picture of him. In the first weeks after my boy was taken from me, there were so many emotions I went through. I was alone with just my thoughts. For the first six months, I cried openly every day. People started telling me I need to move on. So then I avoided people so they wouldn't have to see me cry. When I saw any police, I felt sick to my stomach. I slept so little because of the nightmares. I didn't leave my house, I couldn't. I tried but I would have panic attacks thinking something was going to happen to my other babies. I had nightmares every night for at least a year. I would wake up crying for my boy. I bought books on pet loss and grief. I joined groups on social media for pet loss. I lit candles and put his name on memorial sites on the internet. I thought something must be wrong with me, I didn't think the grieving process should take so long. I felt so alone and I felt nobody out there knew how I felt. Nothing helped lessen the pain in what was left of my heart. The fifth anniversary of Dexter's murder is coming close. I still have nightmares sporadically, more at this time. I believe the grief wouldn't be this hard if he hadn't met such a violent end. We were robbed of his golden years, robbed of memories that could have been. We didn't get a chance to mark anything off our bucket list. I feel selfish because I can't say I'm grateful for the time we had because I want my boy back. I can't say at least we had this time or that because we were robbed of so much more.

There are things about my boy I don't want to ever forget. To forget makes me think I'll forget him. But I know really, I could never forget my Dexter. We were a part of each other. He has a piece of my heart that can never be filled by another. I know my heart has learned to live with the pain, otherwise, I would not have been able to write this.

I love and miss you, Dexter, to the moon and back. I would give the world, if it were mine, to have you back with me again.

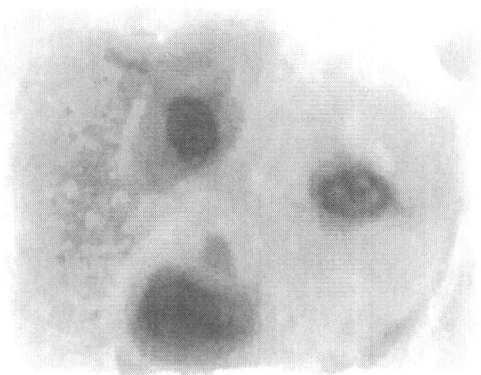

Dexter

For The Love of Milo
By Barbara McComsey

Milo was a seven-year-old boxer and bully mix who found a forever home after being a rescue pup downriver from Detroit. On January 5th, 2009, a cat rescue was looking for cats in a warehouse area and heard cries. When they searched for the cries, the ladies found three puppies abandoned. The thought was that the people who had the mother, took the pups and got rid of them, figuring they were days old, they would die. The cat rescue took in the three pups and cared for them until they were old enough to adopt out. This is where our story begins.

April 2009, my fourteen-year-old son, Brandon, wanted a dog. Not just any dog, he wanted a big dog. We had raised small dogs in my family, Miniature Schnauzers, and I did have my father's Schnauzer, Bugsy, at the time, but Brandon wanted his own pup. I began looking on the Pet Finder page and found a little puppy in a bee suit. He was a velvet tawny brown with white paws, and on the tip of his nose was a white spot that looked like a bow tie. His eyes were so big and brown that they seemed to reach right into my soul. I emailed the rescue and found that he was the last one of the three rescued available. I wasted no time filling out the application.

On a Friday afternoon, I gathered up Brandon and his friend, Joey, and we made our way to a local pet supply store that was also a kitty adoption center for the rescue. It was a perfect place to meet the little pup and see if he was our forever pup. We arrived at the store and as we walked in, this little velvet piggy puppy ran in front of us. Brandon knelt down and the pup ran right for him. We immediately knew he was the one. On the way home in the car Brandon decided to call him Milo, and Milo it was.

Having Milo in the house with his continuous antics, was a breath of fresh air. He was trained very quickly, as he followed my dad's schnauzer, Bugsy, around tirelessly. He ate when Bugsy ate, pottied when Bugsy pottied and slept on Bugsy when Bugsy tried to sleep. They became quick pals.

Brandon was not a typical boy. As a baby, I watched him change. I am in no way saying what a vaccination does or doesn't do, but after Brandon's first MMR injection, I watched a happy baby drift away. He was no longer eager, no longer interested in many toys, and he would watch children's movies over and over. This did not stop as he grew up. School was impossible from the beginning in kindergarten. By first grade, Brandon memorized short reading books and had his teachers believing he was reading them word for word. He memorized them as soon as they were being read to the class. It took most of the year to prove to his teacher that he could not read. At my insistence, the Special education teacher was assigned to my son and there we found that Brandon was dyslexic. During the summer, he was diagnosed with attention deficit disorder, then later with hypo-manic bipolar disorder.

Milo was aware of Brandon's issues and stayed by Brandon's side no matter what the boy was going through. I didn't realize how much in tune Milo was with my son until Easter Sunday 2010, when after a collection of phone calls and anger outbursts, my son walked into the bathroom, closed the door, and began to cut his arms with an X-Acto knife. Milo pawed at the door, whining, which caught my attention and if he hadn't whined, my son would be dead.

Brandon attempted suicide at the age of fifteen. After that incident, I took notice of Milo because he seemed to know what Brandon was going through, even though I saw a somewhat normal, as he could be, young man.

Life seemed to be going along as expected, good days and bad days, but what was to happen next, came out of left field and hit me square between the eyes.

On a beautiful August afternoon, a police car inched past my house, turned around, and parked at the end of my driveway. The first thing that crossed my mind was that they were looking for someone possibly running through the neighborhood. Two policemen walked up to my fence, reached over the post, and began petting Milo. I walked out of my backdoor and greeted them as I would any officer of the law. I asked them if I could be of assistance to them and they notified me that my dog was a pit bull and I laughed. My dog? My dog was a bully breed, yes, the veterinarian identified Milo as an American bulldog, boxer mix.

One of the officers notified me that Milo is indeed a pit bull (such rubbish), and if I didn't remove him from the township immediately, when they came back to my premises, they had the authority to confiscate the dog and euthanize him as the township ordinance states.

I immediately told the officer to remove his hand from my dog and get his arm out of my fenced yard and leave my property, for if the dog bit him, that would give him the right to shoot our beloved Milo.

Once the police left, I panicked. What were we going to do? How could they do this? What ordinance? Milo isn't a pit bull, what gives them the right to say he is? I called everyone I could, crying, emotional, angry.

Through some friends, a pro-bono lawyer contacted me taking my case to keep our Milo. Two days later, she contacted me and said because of the way the ordinance is written, we wouldn't be able to win. The description regarding bully breed dogs was so vague, any dog from a Chihuahua to a Great Dane could be misconstrued to be a pit bull or mix IE short hair, brown, black, or white, square jowls, pointed ears, overbite, underbite, and broad chest. All dogs have something on the list.

I was not about to give my dog away. What would Brandon do? What about Milo?

I found out that a neighbor had called the police on us. A neighbor. I talked to all my neighbors and someone was a weasel. How could they do that to us? Milo never hurt anyone.

We had chickens in the road, a rooster crowed every morning in our subdivision. The neighbor to the west of me left his Akita out at all hours of the night in summer and winter and he barked at everything. The neighbor on the east told me she didn't have rabies shots for her two poodles, they didn't even have licenses. The golden retriever across the street would jump the fence into another neighbor's yard who owned a Husky and at least weekly I would hear their owners arguing and threatening to shoot each other's dogs, and I was the bad guy? I also thought my dog could possibly be poisoned as I found new squeaky toys thrown into my yard almost daily. Milo never left my side and never touched one of those squeaky toys. I had had enough by then, so on a crisp autumn day in October 2011, just over a month after the initial police visit, I decided to sell my home, move out, keep my dog, and be rid of the threats bestowed upon me in my own hometown. I would later learn that tickets had to be given to residents who didn't follow the ordinances, then warnings, and court, but I couldn't afford a court case where my dog's life was in danger. Moving was my only option.

During the time that I was dealing with the police, I had formed a Facebook page specifically for my dog to tell whoever wanted to listen about our fight against a breed-specific law (BSL) in my area, and I found BSLs were not new. States, countries, and Canadian provinces all had BSLs against pit bulls and mixes. Sports Illustrated vilified Staffordshire bulldogs in the late 1980s and the case against Michael Vick in the 1990s running a dog fighting ring solidified people's view of a beautiful breed. Because of this vilification, many people who had no business owning pit bulls aided in the news stories about maiming and killing children, attacking people on the streets, and this just wasn't true. Not all bully breeds harm, they would rather lay around, chase balls, or eat treats. Our Milo proved that every day.

On April 1st, 2012, we moved out of our township and moved 25 miles south to an area that understood that any dog can harm, it was the person who trained them, who owned them and if you proved yourself a bad owner, then the city would come out and decide what needed to be done. I have also learned to read city and township ordinances, rules and regulations as I never wanted to be in fear of losing our Milo again. Milo was worth it. He was not just a dog; he was a part of our family and he was a godsend to my son every day.

Milo became a "spokesdog" in the anti-BSL movement. It began with an open forum during a township trustee meeting. I had just moved, but I was invited to speak to the group. I had five minutes to speak my peace and during that time I enlightened the trustees and the chief of police about what their officers did to me, and it was going to stop with me. I would educate anyone who took the time to listen and I vowed I would not drive through the township, I would not purchase any items within the township boundaries and if anyone asked me about moving to their area, I would let them know exactly what I thought of their area...yes it was beautiful, but the underlying inept group of trustees and the police chief was not to be trusted. I was proud to see my few minutes recorded with my facts and information and with that little speech, Milo and I began to receive invitations to area forums, had newspapers and magazines interview us, attended protest walks in Michigan and Indiana, accepted speaking engagements at various city and municipal meetings, and I attended the largest protest walk in Washington, D.C. in May 2014. I was amazed to see people from all over the United States and Canada, from sea to shining sea, come together in front of our nation's Capital to let our legislators know we will not stand down and we will speak for our dogs who have no voice. Over two thousand people attended the walk that day and to meet and greet Milo's followers and other Facebook pet page families, was so very rewarding. Milo's education banner was carried with pride, with love. We made a difference.

On June 30th, 2015, Milo and I moved to South Florida, to help my sister-in-law after my brother's sudden death. We didn't last long with her as her issues stemmed deeper than my brother's death and we parted ways. On November 1st, 2015, I found an apartment that allowed my dog, because the landlord also knew, good owner, good pet, and we settled into a daily regimen of walks and treats, games, and toys.

Life was going well. It was just Milo and me. Brandon was 20 years old when we moved to Florida and he decided to stay in Michigan.

Our partnership was wonderful until March 2016 when I walked into my apartment to find Milo's abdomen huge. I immediately thought of *bloat* and rushed him to his doctor. The technicians worked on him and said, it was not bloat, he was full of fluid around his heart and needed a 24-hour emergency hospital. We took the tests and X-rays and rushed to the referred hospital. The technicians there took Milo in right away and I sat in a room for what seemed to be an hour. Looking back, it was mere minutes, but the veterinarian on service met me in the room. She was a thin, blonde hair, fair-skinned woman of about thirty. She was very stoic and without a missed step she told me Milo's chest and abdomen were full of fluid and it was indicative of cancer, so she needed to put him down immediately. I stared at her and asked, "What did the blood tests show? What color was the fluid?" As I work in a cancer center, I knew a little about testing and such. This lady was angered by my questions, she left the room, and came back in to show me a large 50 cc syringe full of clear, yellow straw-colored fluid.

I knew this was not a sign of cancer and since she had not done any lab tests on him, I was not about to put him down immediately. A young female technician entered the room and I told her that I had to notify my son, as this was his dog, and I couldn't put Milo down without his consent. The doctor and technician agreed to keep him until the morning to see how he responded to the fluid being drained and I could make a decision then.

First thing the next morning, I called the hospital and a new doctor answered my call. This man was a more seasoned veterinarian and told me his evening partner was probably correct because during the night, they ran an echocardiogram; an ultrasound of the heart, and after looking at the video, he agreed that Milo had a tumor in the top chamber of his heart, but he was not near death and he could have some quality time. The morning doctor referred me to a canine cardiologist and I should go there for a second opinion. With the IV still attached to Milo's front leg, we drove 10 miles to the specialist vet hospital and were greeted with open arms and received wonderful treatment. That was a 180-degree turn from the hospital the night before.

The new doctor, Dr. Schneider, viewed the ultrasound and told me it was the worst CD he had ever seen. He wanted to do another ultrasound at no charge to me, so he could properly see Milo's heart. Dr. Schneider came back to me within minutes and told me that my dog wasn't dying. He didn't know what was wrong, but his heart did not have a tumor, nor were there any signs of any masses anywhere. His labs were ok, some things were off, but nothing to fully say our beloved Milo had cancer. He stayed overnight and no more fluid developed. Milo was eating and drinking and could go home.

For the last week of March, Brandon came to visit. Milo and Brandon were happy to see each other. Brandon was relieved to find his dog in good health and they were both inseparable the entire time Brandon was home.

A week later, Brandon left back for Michigan. Within the week, Milo began to retain fluid again. I took him back and forth to his cardiologist as we drained him, he'd get better, then crash. As a last-ditch effort to give Milo a few more quality years, we decided to perform a cardiac window, which meant removing the pericardial sac, which would allow the fluid to drain correctly. The cost was immense, of course, but because Milo's Facebook page made him "famous," his page had upwards of eight thousand followers, so I hoped to pay for the surgery with donations. I applied to foundations for grants, which I received, sold T-shirts, and had two auctions with donated items from other Facebook famous dogs, and collectively we raised enough money for the surgery, plus money for post-surgical doctor visits.

On April 8th, 2016, Milo endured a successful cardiac window surgery and three days later came home with me. I received cards and well wishes from all over the world, and Milo's Facebook page was flooded with posts from thousands of people. Milo was not only loved by Brandon and me, but also by his followers.

Milo seemed to do well as he was on Prednisone for swelling and it was supposed to keep fluid from backing up. The doctor had assured me that his sac was sent for biopsy to Denver, Colorado and everything was negative. He told me Milo would have another three to four good years. I believed it.

On May 2nd I came home from work to find Milo swollen again. I took him to his cardiology hospital and they drained fluid once again. Dr. Schneider put out a call to all cardiologists in the U.S. to discuss Milo's case. No one had any ideas about what was happening and why. Dr. Schneider tried everything to save our Milo. After five more fluid drains were done in less than a week on our pup, he kept filling up faster than I could manage to drive him back and forth to the hospital.

Many of the visits and a lot of the testing was done at no charge to me. The hospital and doctor were more than fair to us. The receptionist took my calls at all hours of the night, I rushed him in, took him home, rushed him back. It was a never-ending circle.

On May 18th I walked into the apartment and found Milo laboring to breathe again and he was swollen so very bad. I resigned myself to the fact that Milo was suffering and I couldn't allow them to stick him with a needle and pull fluid anymore. His ribs were bruised from all the needle sticks and he had a terrible scar that, although it had healed quickly, it still made him look terrible. I made the call to the hospital and I called Brandon.

At 10:30 p.m. while lying in my arms, I watched his eyes close and heart beat slower and slower until he was gone. My friend, Bea, had driven an hour to be with me, so I wasn't alone when Milo ran to the Bridge. I lost myself completely in the room and cried harder than I had ever cried. I still think I may have cried more at the loss of Milo than at the loss of my mother. My son's lifesaver, this pup who was innocent, never harmed a fly, let alone another animal, was laying on the floor wrapped in his favorite blanket. I couldn't stand to watch him be taken away to the back, but I didn't want him to be alone, so my friend, walked with the resident veterinarian to the back until he was put away to be cremated.

To this day the doctor does not have an answer for me. In the end, they called his case, idiopathic pericarditis. He had no answer for me and still uses his case to find an answer.

In hindsight, I believe his heart was broken by Brandon not being with him. He was not the same dog as he was when Brandon was around. He missed his boy.

I do keep in touch with his last hospital technicians, office manager, and doctor.

Milo has been gone for three years now, but his Facebook page has over nine thousand followers and I carry on the work against breed-specific laws in his memory. I did everything I could to save him, the least I could do was continue his work in his name. Today Milo's remains are now placed in my curio cabinet. His pictures and drawings from friends still adorn the shelf.

Milo was our game changer. Because of Milo, I will never own another breed. He taught us the meaning of unconditional love; to speak up when things do not make sense and to fight for what is right. We are the voice for the voiceless and I will not give up the fight against breed specific legislation until every BSL is repealed. The ordinance that involved Milo still stands to this day. The state bill bounces around then is ignored by the state senate. The township has been shown time and time again that the ordinance must change, but they believe the myths and refuse to change it with one excuse after another.

Someday it will be repealed, and I promised Milo that a small pinch of his ashes will be spread across that township's municipal lawn when it does fall.

For Milo.

Milo

Scamper
By Rebecca Jean

I don't recall how she got her name. I don't know how she even came to be ours. See, I was only four when Scamper became part of our family. She came with us when we moved from Menomonie, Wisconsin to Zion, Illinois. Scamper was basically our family dog. But, as I grew older, she and I became close pals. She heard all my secrets and gave me her love and understanding.

Scamper was a small, brown and white terrier. She had a cute, brown face, but her neck all around and underside were white. Her two-front legs were also white, along with the tip of her tail. Her eyes were golden brown. The kind of eyes that trusted and could look into a little girl's soul. Her ears flopped over when relaxed or suddenly stood up when alerted to her surroundings.

Though Scamper was only taught the basic tricks of sit and lay, she was smart. No doubt about that. She seemed to have a knowing, a wisdom about her like an old soul. She just got life. I don't know how else to explain it.

Scamper was my shadow as I explored and played all over Zion. It was the 1960s and Zion was a dry town, a small, safe town where I walked to the lumberyard for scraps of wood to build a fort or played at a local park. She never was on a leash;

no need. A cat or another dog didn't faze her. The only time Scamper showed aggression was with someone wearing a uniform. It was explained to me by my family that a uniformed man holding a cigarette kicked her. I have no memory of that, but clearly, Scamper did.

An old man who lived about five houses over on my block would regularly walk his gray poodle twice a day. Scamper and I would be relaxing in the grass in my front yard, and the old man would come by with his poodle pulling on its leash, barking, and acting quite

crazed. He would yell at me saying my dog had to be on a leash. Somehow, Scamper and I both agreed the leash was exactly where it should be.

My little pal gave us three litters of puppies. My parents would awaken my siblings and me to announce the puppies were born. Her first litter was one adorable, white puppy with a ring around its tail. We named him Junior. It was like Christmas. Seeing the adorable, innocent, and vulnerable babies whimpering as they found comfort next to their mama. Scamper was a good mommy too. Of course, we named the puppies in hopes of somehow keeping them. But, in the end, homes were always found for the sweeties.

We moved to an apartment until our new home was built. Scamper was happy to be with us no matter where we lived. Mom didn't allow Scamper past the kitchen and she seemed to know her boundaries. She would sit with her paws exactly on the line between the kitchen and the living room.

Our family moved into our new home, across the street from the apartments we had lived in. There were four units and my dad managed them all part-time. Scamper would often accompany him, being the faithful and sweet dog she was.

My Aunt Milly died on June 26th, 1969. The funeral was in Menomonie, Wisconsin. We all went up to the funeral, except Scamper and my brother. We were up in Menomonie for several days.

One day, my brother left Scamper out, forgot about her, and left for work. Scamper crossed the street for the apartments in search of my dad. The dog catcher drove by and spied her. Without trying to catch her or return her home, he shot her with a tranquilizer and took her to the pound. She died on July 3rd, 1969, in the dog pound, all alone. We came home from one sad death to another. This was even more heart-wrenching to a little girl who up to this point, had never experienced death. The next day, Scamper would have turned 10. My dad and I went to the police station looking for answers. Apparently, the dog catcher had many complaints against him for his cruel tactics. He shot Scamper with a tranquilizer too powerful for her size.

Even as I write this, fifty years later, my heart breaks. It is too painful to recall hearing she lay on the cement floor, dead from such cruel hands. A man who was scared of dogs shouldn't be allowed in that line of work. Today there would be justice. So I shall like to remember my cute little Scamper the faithful, sweet, and loyal friend she was with all the love she gave our family. She was a good girl, and somehow, I hope she knows that.

Scamper

Brandy
By Heather Baker

I first set eyes on Brandy a week before my birthday in 2003 when my then fiancé picked me up and this tiny little girl popped out of his jacket pocket. I was not expecting it. I have had asthma my entire life and not able to have a dog. I started getting allergy shots in 2002, the same year I got my mom a Chihuahua for Christmas. It was a great way to see if the allergy shots were truly working. I got to puppy sit a lot and fell in love with the breed but never thought I would be getting one anytime soon.

I was not expecting another pet, I moved in with Dan in 2003 and we already had a Lab, a cat, and two rabbits. Brandy was such a friendly quiet puppy. She played with our Lab but was the perfect little puppy. The only issue was housebreaking and as she got older and had an accident you knew the moment you walked in the door, she would have this grin from ear to ear and looking like she did something wrong, she always gave it away. Brandy went everywhere with me when she was young. My mother-in-law made me a tote that was the same colour as Brandy, she was so good she would just sit in her bag and not say a peep. She was the most well-behaved Chihuahua most people have ever met. I could take her to work, store anywhere and nobody even noticed her in the bag. She was the perfect puppy. So much so that multiple people had gotten a Chihuahua after meeting her. A coworker, Rosemary, got a Chihuahua that we are pretty sure was from the same breeder, they were very similar in personality and looked alike as well. My boss also got a Chihuahua a week after meeting Brandy. She was just that charming.

Unfortunately, Rosemary lost Sasha in May of 2019, exactly one year from losing Brandy. In the weeks leading up to Sasha's death, Rosemary and I touched base a lot - I wanted to help as much as possible, yet it was like reliving Brandy's last weeks. One morning I got up and was heading into work and I received a text, *Sasha died, I am broken-hearted.* I knew exactly how she was feeling and I broke down. It was that deep pain in my heart again. I was hoping I could fix it this time and make her live a bit longer, but we lost her. Rosemary now felt like me, like we lost something so special. Will we ever recover?

Brandy was *my* dog. Brandy was almost a year when Dan and I got married when my mother-in-law surprised me with an amazing flower-pup dress for her when she walked down the aisle with our nephew - she stole the show! – and I was happy to have her brighten the day. During our vows, I saw out of the corner of my eye her starting to run towards me; you can hear her in our wedding video, it is so cute. When we went on our honeymoon I wondered if she would even remember us, but when I walked into the house she came crying like I never heard before, she was so excited to see me. My heart was so happy to know she knew I was her person.

Dan used to run every day with our Lab, Brandy would beg at the door to go so bad he started taking her, she was barely eight months but would run her little heart out and loved it. We then moved to our beautiful home that we have now, next to our in-laws. Grandpa especially loved Brandy, unfortunately, his love was shown by food, and no matter how much I complained he would still sneak food over every day for her when I was at work so much that I was beginning to worry about her health.

She wasn't obese, just chunky. She loved her steak. I still worry if her extra weight contributed to her heart disease.

I used to rescue rabbits (still would but lots of rescues now). We had one female that had four babies, Brandy would always want to be with me when I was helping feed some of them. She loved them so much. She was like a little mother. When they got old enough to run through the house she would just watch them.

Brandy was a very active Chihuahua, we didn't want an unsocial, biting Chihuahua that a lot of people think of when they think of her breed. She was timid of children due to a few being very rough with her and from then on she kept her distance from them. Same thing with off-leash dogs that had come after her a few times. Brandy was always on a leash, not that I worried about her going far from me but because of bigger dogs jumping her again, and luckily with the leash I pulled her out of the fight.

She then became very barky towards bigger dogs, rightly so! She would never bite or be aggressive, it was more just a warning. People would look at me like I have a misbehaved Chihuahua, but when you are six pounds and have a 60-pound dog charging at you, you need to figure a way to protect yourself. But that did limit me from taking her to some places, which I hated. I knew she would not harm anyone but we did a lot with small dog groups and we always did a lot of entertaining so she would always be used to other people and dogs she knew. We live on a lake and she *loved* it.

When Brandy was six years old, Dan brought home a little Chihuahua sister for our fifth anniversary. She liked her for the first hour until she realized she was staying and taking some of my attention from her. It took a while but they did bond, they got even closer when we lost our Lab. Brandy was the head of the household, but Bella wanted it and could be very antagonizing to Brandy. Bella was the long-haired, long-legged, slim, friendlier Chihuahua that everyone would "ah" over. Brandy would always come to me when strangers were around. But she was shy, not anything else but that. Once she knew you, she would welcome you into her life.

In 2013, I noticed she was being more standoffish and sleeping more. She was going in for a teeth cleaning and they found a heart murmur when she was nine. I thought it was going to be a benign incidental finding, but I wanted to see a cardiologist just to confirm. Where I live there is only one that is six hours away, so off we went. That day I remember the shocking information I received. I couldn't even ask questions because it was like I was in a bad dream. She had pulmonary hypertension and right and left leaky valves. It was a triple whammy. Everything was mild but they still didn't know how it would progress. I went to my local vet office but Brandy's vet was on maternity leave; her replacement basically said Brandy may have a year. I thought I was going to die. The only suggestion was for her to lose half a pound to put less strain on her heart. I prayed and prayed for five extra years with her. Now I was stern with everyone that fed her treats. I was spending lots of money on expensive dog food and treats thinking I was doing everything right. Luckily, she lost some weight and at her six-month follow-up nothing had changed so we were on the right track. We would continue to get good news for the next few years, no meds, no change in health. I thought we were doing everything right.

With us living on a lake, she loved being on the water - not so much in it but if there was a float or boat she could jump on she was on it. She would even get on the Sea-Doo with me. Winter was the same, she hated the cold of course but first snow she was out for one quick run. She was such a strong Chihuahua. We have a small property but she would always head to the end of the property which became "Brandy's point." I plan on getting a sign for it. She would graze down there all the time. When I see my new puppy run down there, it reminds me of Brandy.

We live on a small dirt road with the in-laws next door, Brandy would run over there whenever she had the chance. She knew when they were barbequing and wanted in on it. As I sit here typing, I think of the spot next to me that was hers, the chair that had a blanket and was always ready for her. If Bella or our cat was there and she wanted up, they had to get down and make room for Brandy. She was my shadow.

This six-pound little Chihuahua could keep up with my husband even at 10+ years old. We would go to beaches and she would just run and run. Nothing stopped her. She could outrun me right to the end. I am healthy and active but running never was my thing. I now was supposed to not let her get overexerted while running with her heart disease, with me that never happened. She always wanted to keep up with Dan and Bella (who could run like a racehorse with her long legs). In the summer of 2016 I let her out, they went running to chase the birds and I saw Brandy drop, I thought she fell. By the time I got there, she was up and running back. It happened again a few days later, I ran to her, but she was flat on her side and not moving. I thought she was having a heart attack. A few seconds later she came around. I made an appointment and off to the cardiologist for another echo in September. Again, more bad news. Things had progressed enough that it was time for medication. All I could think about was this was the beginning of the end. I was devastated all over again. But we got her on the medication and she was full of energy again and back to herself.

December 16th, 2016 is when life changed. We came home from a fabulous Christmas dinner with my boss and found Brandy not herself. Up until this day I had two other scares with Brandy that I thought it was her heart due to her rapid breathing and pacing; both were on Christmas Day (2014, 2015) and both were from constipation due to too much food. Family dinner was always at my house and how can you resist a cute little face begging for turkey. But when numerous people are giving this six-pound girl food, sometimes it causes trouble. As we were leaving for dinner that night, I thought Brandy was constipated again but she wasn't. I curled up on the couch when we got home with her for a few minutes and all of a sudden she started choking. I thought she was dying in my arms. We jumped in the car and headed to the vet's emergency, she was seizing. We get there and she had stopped but was very disoriented and was like she didn't know who we were. The vet checked her over and told us it may never happen again, so we went home. Ten minutes after being home it happened again, this time we decided to leave her at the vet emergency in case anything happened they would watch her. I normally never left Brandy at the vet because she would become so stressed, I was always worried about her heart. But she didn't even seem fazed by us leaving. This was around 1:00 a.m. We went home and tried to get a few hours of sleep. I picked her up at 8:00 a.m. the next morning, she was very tired but had no issues through the night. They said to take her to our vet immediately to have a workup. When we got there, it was very noisy and set Brandy into another seizure, they kept continuing. They told me they would keep her and be in touch. I wish I would have kept her home that morning, I think the added stress was too much. That afternoon my vet call and said it wasn't looking good. I took off to the vet. They suggested euthanasia. We decided to bring her home and see how it went. She was given medication and hoped for the best. Those next few days I didn't sleep. She was in someone's arms most of the time. If you put her on the floor or bed she would just circle. They said that meant a brain tumor and it would only get worse, they gave her at the most three to four months. December 18th was Dan's birthday, we were only celebrating that Brandy was still with us and holding her own. I was just hoping to have her not in pain and she seemed to be in no pain.

My husband got to work from home while I went to work for a few days. On December 22nd, I got a text with a video of Brandy walking straight and almost herself again. Christmas day she was back to herself, I believed in miracles.

Brandy was still on medications, we saw a neurologist but due to her heart, no diagnostics could be done. It could be a brain tumor or something else. I asked if there is anything we should change or watch out for and she said to let Brandy live her life but she should stay on the meds to assure it doesn't happen again. She was back to her new self and had no seizures, life was good but always guarded. We took her to beaches and had walks; she was happy. Every month that went by was a good one, I didn't go on any vacations or any trips with Dan as he traveled a lot for work. I was afraid something would happen when I wasn't there. I won a weekend trip and Dan told me to go. Of course, Brandy started having major diarrhea before I went away. I almost canceled the trip. One of the medications she was on was Prednisone, a steroid that made her very hungry, so much so that she got into some feces (this has never happened before). Off to the vet. They told me it was Giardia. Due to her low immune system, it took almost two months to clear it up. I felt so bad for her. She could not control her bowels and she was embarrassed.

We hit a year and Dan and I thought that the seizures last Christmas were a one-time thing. Christmas was great, we had the usual company. I got up late on Dec 29th and went downstairs, asked Dan if he gave Brandy her medication. He said, no, so I gave it to her and we curled back on the bed to watch TV. About 20 minutes later, Brandy started seizing again so I rushed her to the vet. That afternoon, a call came in telling me she wasn't stopping the seizures. When I got there, they were happening every 20 minutes. I stayed for hours hoping they would break, but my vet said it was time. We were going to euthanize at home after she got off work around 7:30 p.m. Dan came upstairs with some chicken for her. We got a pill into her and she stopped seizing at 7:00 p.m. It wasn't her time yet, but we were starting from scratch again and this time she was slower to respond; she had focal seizures but we got them under control. More medications for my little girl. We kept her on strong seizure medications because the vet figured it was her brain tumor growing and she would need them. A few months went by and she was fine still, but this time her liver functions were high. It was the new meds. We had to get her off them fast. I was terrified. I don't know if I had a solid sleep in 2018, with all my thinking of her seizing and dying. Now the focus is to make sure she doesn't go into kidney failure.

My thoughts were not with her heart issues at this point, it was the seizures and liver functions until April 6th. I had just emailed my vet that evening saying how good she was feeling again finally and we had been outside to visit the in-laws, she was doing great. Then around midnight, she started breathing heavily, it would start and stop all night. I was going to take her to emergency but it would come and go and I figured I would just go to my vet at 7:00 a.m. We get there and her lungs had fluid in them. They then put her on Lasix. What if I would have taken her the night before, would it have gotten that bad? I question a lot going forward.

Over the next few days, she was up and down. I told them I didn't think the Lasix was working so they gave me more meds. I asked if we should go to the cardiologist, but she said they would give her the same things. I called the cardiologist anyway, but he was away. She should have had an appointment in February/March but we were so worried about the liver function and getting her off the seizure meds I was afraid to put her in a car for six hours and endure an echo during this time. I probably should have done it anyway. Saturday, April 14th, she was struggling so much that she had a seizure. We had the meds to stop it but I took her to the vet anyway because she was still struggling. It wasn't my regular vet, but again another medication – she wanted me to euthanize. I said you don't know how strong this little girl is, she has beat death a few times.

Brandy started to improve but she still wasn't eating much. I cooked her everything I could think of, but it also was a struggle getting all these pills in her. She was up and down for the next few days. She had an appointment for bloodwork on April 18th. That day I could see she was struggling again. We went to the vet and the stress of the wait and the appointment itself, she was in bad shape. The vet said there was nothing she could do, I begged for anything. She said it was time. I broke down crying on the floor. Brandy came up to me, licked my face and stopped coughing. She didn't want to see me heartbroken. Brandy walked out of the vet's office like there was nothing wrong. She did it for me, she did it to stop me from crying.

That night I slept on the couch in the living room with her, I was terrified she was going to die. She was restless and walked around. I got up and went to work early, I was going to come home at 1:30 p.m. and figure out our next step – a new vet or what to do – I was so tired; I could imagine how Brandy felt.

I got a webcam when Brandy first started seizing so I could keep an eye on her, and during those two weeks I did more staring at the webcam than working. But Brandy always pulled out of it.

I was getting ready to leave work when I could see she was struggling, How do you tell your boss again that you have to leave because of your dog? I get a frantic text from my husband, *COME HOME NOW!* I ran out of work and called him while driving. I could hear him screaming, "No Brandy, *no* Brandy.*"* Then he said, "Don't rush, it's too late." My heart and soul left me that day. I have not felt the same since.

I got home and Dan was on the floor holding Brandy. I took her, she just looked like she was asleep. I held her for hours, I didn't want to let her go. My heart would leave with her. I put her in her bed, she looked peaceful, but it just wasn't real. My friend came over with a beautiful, decorated box and bed she picked up on the way over. We put her in it and kept her in our garage. I would go out and look at her over the next few days until Dan dug a deep hole in my garden for her, I didn't want to bury her - that makes it final. I am sure the neighbours heard me scream as we put her in the ground and covered her, it was the end.

The next week I was like the walking dead, I had no feeling, no heart, I was just hollow inside. Poor Bella was confused and sad too. She was waking me up in the middle of the night to go outside. I thought she had to pee but she was looking for Brandy. She was going to her favourite spots and sniffing, nothing else. She had a rough year. X-rays looked good but I think the combination of the loss of Brandy and arthritis was hard for her. She was getting better with meds but she was due for a teeth cleaning and I was terrified, she was 10 years old and has a heart murmur.

I still question about burying Brandy – should I have cremated? I would have her with me forever, I question if I should have had a necropsy to help with my grief and guilt, but could I do that to my little girl?

I do have a beautiful headstone for her grave. That isn't enough though, I want something more to remember her with, something to have with me all the time. Do I get my first tattoo at the age of 53? I don't make rash decisions so right now I am looking at a piece of jewelry.

I question everything – if she wouldn't have gained weight or had the "designer" kibble, would she have gotten heart disease? Did I cause the seizures? I had essential oils that nobody told me not to use after she had the seizures. They were so sure it was a brain tumor but I don't think it was. Was it me giving the second dose of medications that day to cause her to have them? What if I would have went to the cardiologist a month earlier, would she have been put on more meds and got stable?

So, here I am in September 2019. She would have been 16 on September 10th. I know that sounds old but Chihuahuas live longer. My mom's Chihuahua, Max (the original), will be 17 next month. He was fed bacon and chicken every day, no exercise and other than losing his hearing is healthy. He just had his teeth cleaned last month.

Within days of Brandy's passing, Dan wanted to "fix things" by getting a new puppy. I really didn't want one but I knew if I didn't do some research he would come home with one. I wanted another Chihuahua of course and I messaged a local breeder. I wanted to be on the list for a summer puppy which would give me some time to grieve. She said that she did have one due in that time period but she also had this puppy that was now up for adoption because the owners wanted a guarantee she would be under four pounds and the breeder said she could not guarantee that. She was considering keeping the puppy and had named her Brandy. We chatted back and forth for a bit and we went to look at her. I wanted her but was my heart ready, was Bella ready?

On May 24th, a month after I lost Brandy, we brought her home. I had a few names but settled on a name to memorialize Brandy. Sky is here because Brandy is in the sky watching over us. She was one pound and seven ounces of cuteness but it took me a bit to bond, I felt like I was cheating on Brandy. In early July I broke my arm and had to have surgery. When I went under anesthesia, they told me to think of something that I wanted to dream of for a long time. I thought of Brandy. The surgery went great and I was home with Sky and Bella for a few weeks, they were my couch buddies. I couldn't have made it through 2018 without them. Bella is feeling better and Sky, well she is a very unique Chihuahua. My husband is madly in love with her and she does no wrong. Sky is very outgoing and social and wants to give you all her love and kisses. My dog trainer even said she is one of a kind.

Her personality is different than Brandy but when I see her running or certain actions, I see a bit of Brandy in her. I must say it does make me smile.

I don't know if the pain and guilt will ever go away but I know the time I had with her is hard to just put into words. I know I am not alone now. I had to go to counseling because I felt like I couldn't get through a day without crying my eyes out and I feel like all my friends were tired of listening to me. I do know that I feel like a different person, my soul feels different. I have never cried so much in my entire life as I have since April 19th, 2018. I guess that means Brandy left a huge impression on my heart, she also left a big hole that will always be there for only her. My first dog, the six-pound love of my life taught me more than most humans could. I hope I didn't let you down too much, Brandy, you were my world for 14.5 years but will always be with me.

Brandy

My Angel in Disguise
By Cari N. Cook

"No more Brittanys!" That's what I said for nine long years. In September 2006, our wedding gift was an eight-week-old Brittany puppy. We were ecstatic to have him in our life. My husband came from a family that hunted pheasants and had Brittanys, and I came from a family that loved and spoiled our dogs. I just knew I wanted a dog as soon as I moved out of my mother's house. Having a Brittany puppy was going to be so much fun. All my in-law's Brittanys were named after alcohol. This one wasn't going to be any different. His name was to be Triple Malt Scotch on the Rocks or Scotch for short.

Many people thought he was a springer spaniel growing up, as he is mostly liver and white. He was hard to house train but never had an issue in our bed. Whenever my husband went to work in the morning, Scotch got to come in and sleep with his momma. To this day, he still loves sleeping under the covers. He even had a rabbit friend that he left alone for the first year.

When Scotch was almost a year old, we got him a little brother. He was a Peke-a-Poo named Casey, and unfortunately, they couldn't play with each other for the first month because Casey was just too small at two and a half pounds. After that first month though, Casey pinned Scotch all the time to the floor. He was so gentle with Casey and other small dogs.

After the first couple of years with Scotch, I started to learn what my husband meant when he said they are a one-person dog. He would take him hunting and he would only mind him. I was hoping he would be a momma's boy, but that was a big no. He developed such a stubborn attitude that I just couldn't stand to be around him anymore. He never listened to me. I started to tell my husband, "It's me or the dog!"

Year after year, I kept saying no more Brittanys. My husband could choose another breed to hunt with. I just wanted a breed who actually listened to me. I even have back problems and I couldn't even walk him anymore. Anytime I take him somewhere, he has to have on a shock training collar so I can handle him. He just acted like I wasn't even around. At that point, I'm glad I had Casey, my little Peke-a-Poo, to love on and spoil. They played all the time but Scotch still didn't mind me at all.

Over the years, he became a fat grumpy old man. I was still saying, no more Brittanys in 2016. The time came when my father-in-law was looking for a Brittany himself, and I started helping him find a breeder. I was bound and determined to make sure it was a reputable breeder. I happened to find one that was offering two male Brittanys for a fairly cheap price, as they were already five and a half months old. Low and behold, the breeder happened to have bred Scotch's mom. These puppies came from good hunting and show lines. I tried talking my father-in-law into going and looking at them because the price was down, just so they could find a good hunting home. He never went. However, we went and looked, and sure enough, I couldn't leave without one of the puppies. He was perfect for me. I got myself a Brittany puppy.

What did I get myself into? We needed a name that said alcohol but was also easy to call in the field. He became Bailey No Irish Cream, Bailey for short. The *No* was added because for the first few weeks, we were always saying, *Bailey no...Bailey NO*. It just seemed to fit. Bailey is mostly orange with orange mixed in the white called roan. He is gorgeous.

I was a stay-at-home mom at the time and home every day with Bailey. This time, I was going to have a Brittany that was a momma's boy. He followed me everywhere and slept with me on the couch. I was bound and determined to make him mine.

When Bailey was just over a year old, I took him to his first field trial. If I was going to make him mine, then we were going to compete. Unfortunately, we came in last place, but that's because instead of finding the pheasant like he was supposed to do, he wanted to be always in sight of his momma. I'm just glad the judges on horseback didn't bother him. He just bothered me by not doing what he was supposed to be doing.

He sure is my trickster dog though. He knows his basic commands, but the one thing you need to know is his balancing trick. Bailey hates it but does it for his momma. He will balance up to six toys or five treats on his head. It all started with his favorite toy, a stuffed pheasant. The toy has no tail or wings, but he will still balance it every time I ask. He even sleeps with the thing in his mouth.

I suffer from multiple mental health issues. Besides trying to get him into field trials, I was determined to make him a psychiatric service dog for anxiety, depression, and bipolar disorder. With all my issues, he would make the perfect service dog. Let's begin the training.

Some things he picked up pretty quickly while others took some extra training. The best thing he learned was how to block. I was not comfortable with hugs from people, unless I wanted one, and he learned to stand in front of me to block someone from getting too close. I was doing the training all on my own. I even bought him an awesome-looking vest and started to take him places for extra training in public. The vest was teal to match his collar and leash, and it has awareness ribbons for mental health on it.

During the whole training aspect, my husband didn't believe in mental health issues. He refused to let Bailey come anywhere for any kind of training, yet I needed Bailey the most when I was with my husband. He just wouldn't help out with the training and always under-minded what I already had trained Bailey to do.

I started training him to do deep pressure therapy (DPT). That is when he lays on me to keep me still from the shaking and to get my mind off of the current problem. Little things will make me cry easily with my anxiety and Bailey gets right in my face if I start one little sniffle. Now, if I even cough, he is just inches away from my face trying to figure out what is going on with his momma. He wants to make sure his momma is ok.

In November 2018, I thought it was time to let myself go. My husband and I were in counseling, and I just couldn't take life anymore. So I tried it. I put a bag over my head and slowly started to pass out and leave this world. Out of nowhere, this faint sound woke me up, and it was Bailey jumping on our couch beside me. Right then and there, I was awake and telling myself to stop. From that point on, little things still make him get in my face. I believe that he felt me slipping away that night and God knew it wasn't time. Even when I take all my medicine, I feel he is there counting all the pills I take at one time, to be sure it's the right amount.

If it wasn't for my Bailey, I wouldn't be here today to write about him. He is too shy to use as a service dog now, but my next dog will be one. My husband now knows what Bailey truly means to me and what mental illness is.

Yes, Casey was jealous at first, but now they are brothers and inseparable. They sleep together and eat together. They play and roughhouse. They both protect their momma.

I never wanted another Brittany. They are too high-strung and shed far too much. Brittanys only listen to one person and tolerate the other. Bailey is higher strung than Scotch and sheds far worse, but boy does he listen to me.

Bailey, *my* Brittany, is truly my angel in disguise.

Bailey

Over the Bridge and Back Again
Cari N. Cook

Stormy was an amazing boy. So, let's start at the beginning. May 1999, I was at the end of seventh grade in Ohio when my mom and I decided it was time to get another dog. Our current girl, Taffy, was older and slowly declining. She was already 15 and we didn't know how long we had with her. Little did we know, there was a special little boy being born that very month.

We found a two-year-old Yorkshire terrier that needed rehoming, but she was a little bigger than what we wanted. We weren't 100% sure if she was a pure Yorkie. Then, we met a little long-haired Chihuahua that was named Stormy. However, the little girl in the family just couldn't let her go, so we left empty-handed. We discussed the Yorkie and possibly getting a puppy instead. We went back and forth with the family about the Chihuahua, but they decided they were going to keep her.

My mother and I already discussed the fact that we wanted a non-shedding dog. She found an ad in the local paper for something called a Peke-a-Poo, but all they had were males left and we wanted a female. We went to look anyway, just for the heck of it.

It was the middle of July 1999, and we met two little black balls of fluff. One had curly hair like a poodle and the other

115

had wavy hair. Yes, he was a male, but that tiny wavy-haired little boy followed me all over the yard. That was it. He was coming home with us. Remember that Chihuahua's name? No, we didn't forget either. Stormy.

He was a tiny little thing that had to sleep with me his very first night. We had a 1980s big, old-square playpen that was perfect for him. It fit his crate to sleep in and plenty of newspaper to potty on. Let's just say he never slept in there at night again…no matter how hard I tried. If we left to go somewhere, he stayed in the playpen, but by the time he was housetrained, he was already jumping out of it on his own. Such a silly boy.

We both believe that he was the reason that our Taffy stayed healthy. We noticed that after her sight had gone, she would follow him closely up a ramp and into the house. She just sensed him, and it kept her going. She was a Lhasa apso-Pomeranian mix, who looked more like a Pomeranian-Chihuahua mix.

Stormy loved people and other dogs. All we had to ask was, "Do you want to go see Hershey?" He would get all excited to go visit my sister and her chocolate Lab. We always joked they were boyfriend and girlfriend. It got to the point he started knowing his way to their house and would start to cry well before we ever asked. He loved car rides and would never think twice about going on one. I'm fighting back tears writing this.

Taffy was really declining at this point and my mom knew she wanted another dog to ease her emotionally once Taffy was gone. Taffy was older than me and her declining health was hard on both of us.

Then came another newspaper ad in December 2000, bichon poodle mixes. Oh wow, we love bichons, and we already have a poodle mix. Great, they'll be close in age. We go and pick up the runt of the litter and name him Kodi. At this point, we now have three dogs, a sixteen-year-old, a one-and-a-half-year-old, and now a new puppy. It was a little odd at first growing up with only one dog and then having three in over a year. When March 2001 came, we knew it was time. Taffy had to go over the Bridge. But this story isn't about her. I wish I remembered more about her though.

As I grew older and went to high school, Stormy and Kodi became brothers. Stormy would chase Kodi around the couch and Kodi would duck under while Stormy still went in circles. We would come home and he would have to grab a toy, squeaking it up and down the hallway and talking the entire time. He was such a mouthy little boy. He had to sleep with at least one foot on me at all times; he had to know where I was all night long.

Shortly after I got my license, I got him certified as a therapy dog. I knew he loved people and would enjoy visiting people in nursing homes. However, between school and work, we were never able to visit. I kept his registration going in case we ever got the chance.

He was my bub. I trained him to do so many tricks. He learned that I always did them in order, so if I pointed to the floor, he would do them all, not without a little back talk of course. He sat, laid down, rolled over, backed up, danced, and so many other things. If I woke up after my mom did, Kodi would still be in bed under the covers. Stormy wouldn't say good morning to her until he found Kodi and got him out of bed.

Nothing bothered this boy. He loved his car rides and even traveled to Evart, Michigan, and to Shanksville, Pennsylvania, where Flight 93 went down on 9/11. We went camping every year and he loved to ride on a pontoon boat. He didn't like the water but loved having his ears blow in the wind. Anytime I rode in the car with my mom, Kodi would ride in the middle between us and Stormy would ride in the back. He would often put his head on my shoulder, as it was his way of asking me to come up. Oh, how I miss that feeling.

Then came the day I was to move out and move on with my life. It was September 2006, and I had just gotten married. Stormy was only seven but I knew I couldn't separate him and Kodi. They were brothers and it wouldn't be fair. I said I would never live without a dog and I had fallen in love with a Peke-a-Poo. He even spent the night a few nights with me in our house.

Our first dog as a married couple was a Brittany named Scotch. What a surprise that was. I was raised with small dogs that didn't shed and now I have this crazy breed that sheds a *lot*, but that's a story for another time. Now, six months later in 2007, my husband and I moved to Michigan and had to leave my Stormy behind, but he was with Mom and Kodi, so I knew he was safe.

Not long after, I found the same breeder of Stormy and found she had a little that was just born. How awesome. They were born the same day, May 13th, as my Stormy. I knew it was meant to be. On July 5th, 2007, I drove down to Ohio and picked up this little, tiny man Peke-a-Poo I named Bosco. If you ever watched the show Third Watch, he was named after Jason Wiles' character, Maurice "Bosco" Boscorelli. The perfect little Peke-a-Poo, caramel-colored with black on his face and ears.

We visited my mom the next weekend and Stormy and Bosco played and played. Bosco loved playing with his big brother Scotch and his uncle Stormy.

Bosco, unfortunately, is a story for another time as well. His won't be as long. You see, on Scotch's first birthday, July 21st, 2007, Bosco was attacked. He was only a day shy of 10 weeks old. I only had him for two and a half weeks. That's why his story wouldn't be long. This one is about my bub, my Stormy.

Right after Bosco crossed the Bridge, a new little six-week-old Peke-a-Poo came into my life. He was so tiny but I knew I would protect him at all costs. Casey is now almost 12 and a total brat, but I wouldn't have it any other way.

Casey knew him as Uncle Stormy and would get excited to visit him, or he visit us. They would play and play. They were so much alike, except Casey is blonde and Stormy is black with a white chest. Casey has a long, curly-haired tail and Stormy had a little nub that they docked. Stormy was a little stocky at 18 pounds and Casey is slim but tall at 15 pounds. Either way, I have found that Peke-a-Poo dogs tend to be the same in personality and temperament. I could go on and on about Casey. I just love him so much.

The best time was when I house sat in 2010. My mom went on a trip and I stayed with Stormy and Kodi, with my Casey, of course. We played and played. I took some amazing photos of him running and posing. Little did I know.

During this time, my sister was living with my mom and they found that Stormy would hide behind the couch at times, but they couldn't figure out why. He wouldn't always do this, but it was still a strange behavior. We now know what it was all about. He was hurting.

During Christmas, I decided to tell my family I was expecting. What a shock that was for them. I didn't mention this, but boy did Stormy love opening presents. Stormy helped my mom open her grandma gift. No presents could be left out at Christmas as he thought every present was for him. He never ate the paper but loved to shred it with the boxes. He was so good. I didn't know this would be the last time I would see him.

He was 11, but still a rambunctious little boy. He loved my sister's boyfriend and would hang out with him any chance he got. He was still a wild boy and an outside dog at heart.

On February 21st, 2011, that crazy boy got groomed. Oh, now there's a story. He *loved* going to the groomer. He was her first dog to ever hang out on her desk. I've never seen a dog love his groomer as much as he did.

It was now February 22nd, I was talking to my mother and she said Stormy was throwing up a little and not drinking much water. We figured it was just something that he ate running around the groomer's house. At least, that's what we were hoping.

Wednesday night, February 23rd, I received a text message from my sister, *Do not tell Mom I am texting you, but I'm here to tell you that Stormy is not good. The whites in his eyes are starting to roll up.* Just then, another text message from my sister said our mother was calling an emergency vet who was 45 minutes away. The whole time I am becoming very restless and stressed. Not to mention, I was 14 weeks pregnant. My sister's fiancé and our mother arrived at the vet. They quickly took him back for an ultrasound, X-rays, and blood work. The doctor thought it might be something with his kidneys, which was treatable. That's what we wanted to hear.

They were in the exam room when the vet tech gave something to Stormy to help relieve his pain. Just then the vet came in and stated that his blood work was telling them that he was in complete liver failure. That was the one thing we didn't want to hear. My mother said he was becoming unresponsive, even to my sister's fiancé, who was his best friend for the last two years.

At 1:30 a.m. on February 24th, 2011, I was on the phone with my mother and I made the decision to have him put down. That was the first time I ever had to make that kind of a decision, additionally, it was over the phone and four hours away. At 1:53 a.m., I received a text message from my mom stating, *He's at peace, we're taking him home*. He was only 11 years old.

That day, I took off work. There was no way I could go in. My mom drove the four hours up to bring him to me, so I could say goodbye. I didn't know how. He was already gone, and all that was left was his body. I couldn't let him go. There was just no way he could be gone. I wanted to have him cremated so he would always be with me, but I just couldn't see him going into the fire.

As I sit here and write this, I can't help but think how much fun he would've had in our backyard at our new house and with our daughter. He was truly one of a kind. He will always be missed and always loved. He is buried under a lilac bush with Taffy, Bosco, and three wonderful cats that he grew up with (and Kodi too).

Stormy was my Bub. A name I often called him as a mixture between Baby and Buddy.

I know he will be there waiting with all of them, for when we enter Heaven.

But the story doesn't end here. After Stormy passed, my mom got a Shih Tzu named Cooper. He is an ornery little boy. As time passed, Kodi did too. He was 15 years old. An age we were certain Stormy would live to see.

Cooper needed a brother as he was lonely when my sister moved out. What happens when you see "free to good home" on Facebook? Yup, you guessed it. I drove to Ohio and the next day my mom and I were on a road trip to Chicago to pick up a Shih Tzu mix named Chevy.

Chevy is an amazing dog. He talks when you have his toy. He plays with toys when you walk in the door. He lays his head on my mom's shoulder in the car, asking if he can come into the front seat. He does it all, he is Stormy.

Stormy

The Magic of Maya and Me
By Chantal Barralis

Love at First Sight

When my first baby, Tiffany, passed away in August 2000, I was so heartbroken that I never thought I would get another cat again. Then one month later, I was walking in the street in Nice and passed in front of a pet store's window; there was this beautiful Siamese Seal Point kitten with gorgeous blue eyes. I went in to meet her and as soon as the saleswoman put this beauty in my arms, I instantly fell in love. She started to lick my face like crazy and purred very loudly. From that moment, I knew she was meant to be my little princess. I was living with my parents back then and we had a dog, Bingy, so I needed to ask their permission first before buying this beautiful kitten. I didn't want to do it on the phone so I went all the way back home so I can activate my puppy eyes to convince them to allow me to get her. As soon as they gave me their blessing, I ran back to the pet store, praying that no one had taken her already. Luckily when I arrived, she was still available. As a Siamese, she was very expensive, so I had to write three checks to be cashed every month. She was constantly meowing during our walk home. Once we arrived, Bingy just wanted to play with her and she got a bit scared and even started hissing at him. We had to find a name for this sweet little baby. I wanted something exotic so my mom came up with Maya and that became her name.

Maya would not let me sleep during our first night together. She kept jumping all over me and kept licking my face, it was like she was saying thank you for giving her a loving home. As days went by, Maya was getting used to Bingy and they would play and sleep with each other.

After a week of having Maya, I noticed that she was a little bit pink in some areas so I brought her to the vet. He confirmed to me that she had ringworm. She lost patches of fur and the treatment was very long and expensive. I told the pet store owner that she was sick, hoping that she will help me pay the vet bills but no, all she offered was to take Maya back and give me another kitten. No way. She was my cat and belonged with me. I can only imagine what would have happened to her if I gave her back.

Life with Maya

Maya was such a smart, loving, and sweet cat. She was so beautiful with piercing blue eyes. She would greet me every day when I got home from work by meowing and rubbing all over me. She loved to play fetch with balls. Sometimes I thought she was more a dog than a cat! She would sleep with me every night and if I was ever late, she would go on top of the bed and start meowing until I joined her. She knew when I was sad and knew exactly how to make me smile again. We had this special unbreakable bond in between us, it was like magic.

Big Move to the US

We had a great life in Nice with my parents and Bingy but in November 2007, I decided to move back to New Jersey. There was no way I would let Maya travel in cargo so I called Delta Airlines and made sure she would be able to travel with me in the cabin. On the morning of the flight in March 2008, I was so nervous for many reasons but I was mostly afraid of how Maya would react on the plane. It went really well, she just got a bit sick and meowed when we were landing. She was such a brave little girl.

It took her a few days to get adapted to her new surroundings but soon she started to love my boyfriend with whom I was living with at the time.

For many years it was just Maya and me, she was my rock. My life revolved around her and I wouldn't dare to date anyone who was allergic to cats because she would always come first.

She would love to take Sunday naps in my arms under her favorite blanket. Ever since we moved to New Jersey, she enjoyed going out on a leash and would love to smell the grass.

Cancer Scare

In November 2012 I noticed Maya was a bit lethargic when I came home from work. After picking her up I noticed this huge red bump on her rear end. I went to the vet right away and they scheduled surgery for the very next day. They prepared me saying that it could be cancer and if it is, the placement is most likely fatal. My heart just stopped and I started to cry. I couldn't sleep that night because I was just so worried. It turned out to just be an anal gland abscess and Maya was sent home with the cone of shame and some antibiotics.

Maya's Senior Years

Maya stayed playful for many years and always had a great appetite. She did start to walk slower and slept a lot. She would still climb on my shoulders. I would bring her to the vet to get her geriatric blood work done every year and it has always come back normal. She did lose all of her teeth even though I would brush them quite often, I guess like humans, there's nothing we can do against aging. I thought she was going to live forever or at least make it until 20 years old.

Fight Against Kidney Disease

In January 2019, I brought Maya to the vet for her geriatric bloodwork. She would still eat like a pig, go to the bathroom, and seemed happy. She had lost some weight but I didn't think it was alarming. The vet took her blood pressure and it was perfect so there weren't really any signs of any illness.

I'll always remember the day the vet called me while I was at work to give me Maya's bloodwork results. I can still hear those dreadful words, "Stage three of kidney disease." The vet told me that Maya would need subcutaneous fluids to be administered every day at home. That same night I went to the animal hospital so they could give me the fluids and show me how to do it. I was a bit scared because I didn't want to hurt Maya but it turned out to not be too difficult and Maya was very easygoing. I also had to give her renal diet food and luckily she liked it.

After doing the fluids for about a month, I noticed Maya was eating a bit more and seemed to be doing well. We did blood work again and her kidney disease had regressed. I was so happy. The fluids were working and Maya would still have many years to live.

Then one day in March she stopped eating and meowed when I would give her the fluids. I knew something was wrong. I also noticed that her breathing wasn't normal so I brought her to the vet. We did an ultrasound scan of her kidneys and the vet said they looked really good so she decided to do some in-house bloodwork on Maya so we can get the results right away. While we were waiting, I told her about the abnormal breathing, that I knew Maya and I can tell something is wrong. The vet did an ultrasound of the heart and unfortunately, she discovered fluids around it. Just then, the results were ready and it turned out that her kidney values went up again; there was nothing we could do as I couldn't give fluids anymore to Maya or else her heart would be even more damaged, and I couldn't treat her heart because of her kidney disease. The vet told me Maya had at most two weeks left to live. I didn't want to believe it and just started sobbing. When we came back home, I remember dropping to my knees and kissing her, telling her she wasn't allowed to leave me.

The next day, I saw that Maya was trying to eat a little so I had hope and decided to go see a cardiologist.

Unfortunately, the animal hospital had no appointments available until May and advised me to come the next day to the ER and there I would be able to see one. That night I decided to sing Maya her favorite song and captured it on video. I was so distraught that I mixed the lyrics by singing, "You make me happy when skies are blue," instead of, "You make me happy when skies are grey."

Time to Say Goodbye
On the morning of March 9th, 2019, I brought Maya to the ER. When I put her in the pet carrier, I thought she would be coming back home because she's a little fighter, I had no idea this was going to be her last trip.

When we arrived at the ER, the first thing the vet tech told me was that her body temperature was low. He then took her away to be examined by the vet. The vet came in and told me that there isn't much left to do. Maya's body temperature was low, she had fluids around her heart and lungs and maybe cancer. She said that if I brought Maya back home, she wasn't even sure she would make it through. She asked me to think about it and left the room, telling me when I was ready to make a decision to just press the button and she will come back. The hardest decision of my life. If I was selfish, I would have kept Maya with me as long as possible but she was suffering and was just very good at hiding it. I pressed the button and when the vet came in, I told her while sobbing that the best thing for Maya would be to put her to sleep. She reassured me it was the best decision for her and told me that an office assistant will bring me to a quiet room.

That quiet room was very peaceful. I sat down on the leather armchair with my friend nearby, waiting for the vet to bring in Maya. She comes in and I can see in her eyes that she was done fighting. The vet put her on my lap where I had laid down her blanket. Her body was so cold and her breathing was irregular. I stayed with her for about 10 minutes, taking her last pictures, kissing and petting her. I told her how much I loved her.

The vet came back in and asked me if I'm ready. I say, yes. While petting Maya, who was still on my lap holding onto my thighs, she first injects the sedative. Maya twitches a bit but rapidly goes to sleep. A few moments later, she gives the second injection to make her heart stop. Within 10 seconds, I knew Maya was gone as she let go of my thighs and her arms just slid down. It was all very peaceful. Before taking her away, I kissed her while she was in the vet's arms.

Life Without My Sweet Baby Maya

Maya gave me almost 19 years of endless love. She was my baby girl, my world, and meant everything to me. Losing her just left a big hole in my heart and the first week was very hard for me because I just felt so lost. I couldn't even sleep in my bed because it reminded me of her. I would just lay on the couch, hugging the blanket where she had passed away. I missed hearing her purr and her meow. Then one day I just woke up and felt better. She will never be forgotten but life goes on. I was finally able to look at her photos and watch her videos without crying. All those happy memories brought a smile to my face.

About two weeks later, Maya came back home. Instead of being upset, I felt some sort of relief because she was back home right where she belongs.

In June 2019, I welcomed two male kittens, Phoenix, a Chocolate Lynx Point Siamese, and Hendrix, a Lilac Point Balinese. I know Maya would want me to give a loving home to other kittens and she would want to see me happy because she never liked to see me sad.

I miss you so much my baby, but I know you're still around me in spirit. I will love you forever my little Princess Maya.

-Mommy

You are my sunshine, my only sunshine
You make me happy when skies are grey
You'll never know, dear, how much I love you
Please don't take my sunshine away

Maya

Lady Anne
By Christy Terrill

February 2007 began what we now call a career in rescue. I somehow landed in a pet store on a cold yucky Saturday night and while purchasing fish food ended up taking home a foster dog. Our six-year-old son was ecstatic. This first foster dog was quickly adopted and our next fosters were adopted quickly too. And so it went; get a scared dog needing vet care and kisses to then say goodbye so that it may continue to heal and grow to love their forever family.

Then one day I got a call from the foster coordinator. She wants to know if we are ready to foster a mom dog with four pups that are only days old. With no hesitation, we dove right in. The foster coordinator and I rode to the city pound and brought them to my house where Sweetie and her four pups immediately settled onto the clean comforter in the corner of my kitchen. Two days later we get another call asking us to get a nine-month-old beagle/Boston terrier mix (more on this amazing dog later) who had been surrendered by the previous owner. Owner surrenders in a high-kill facility are first on the list for euthanasia. Getting her out was something that needed to happen as soon as possible. So, we made room for Dede in our dining room. We fell in love with all of them. Sweetie was an amazing mother who took great care of her pups. She allowed Tomas, our son, to hold and snuggle them. Every chance Tomas got he'd pick up the black fluffy one to carry around. She was treated like his most prized teddy bear ever. He called her Black Cutie because he'd just finished the book Black Beauty and that's what she was. This pup was a black beauty.

Fast forward to the time they are ready for their new homes and this particular pup had grabbed the attention of a beautiful young lady far away from Missouri. The family planned a whirlwind round trip drive from Wisconsin to Missouri and back again. I thought they were crazy. But they made it back home with a puppy that had already become a part of their hearts and been renamed the regal name of Lady Anne. (Also note that Lady Anne's mom and siblings all also found great forever homes.) For the next few years, through the magic of social media, my family and I watched Lady Anne and her mom grow up. No vacation, hiking trip, weekend BBQ, or life event was celebrated without a picturesque photo of Lady Anne and her family. We celebrated our love of rescue with every photo. Those photos comforted us during the years following.

Tomas often became disheartened when we lost a pup that couldn't be saved or we had to adopt a pup that had touched our own hearts in a special way. Sometimes just when we needed it most, I would sink into social media to escape, and there would be a regal photo of Lady Anne lounging on a sailboat or framed perfectly alongside her mommy with love shining in her eyes. Do you know the kind of unconditional love only a dog can express? That's what I call my "paycheck." When I see how this mere animal has enriched and completed a person or family, there is just no other. The love that grows as it is shared just, simply, cannot be equaled.

I know this is supposed to be a story of my love, loss, and grief but I felt this story needed to be told from another side. It needs to be known how far-reaching the joy shared with a pet can reach and the impact these fur babies have on all of us. My family and son, now 17 years old, have celebrated the life of Lady Anne. We have also grieved so deeply in our hearts with and for her mom. We do not grieve for Lady Anne because she had the most miraculous life ever. We celebrate that her life was so amazing and special and, well, it was everything anyone could ever hope for in a dog's life!

Dede was the crazy 9-month-old untrained beagle/Boston terrier mentioned earlier. She barreled into our lives with a force I've still not seen in any other dog. Tomas and I had gone to the animal control facility and brought her home. After a quick bath and the most zoomies I've ever witnessed, she began to win over our hearts. But it just wasn't meant to be for her to live with us…yet.

She was adopted by an elderly couple who just did not have the stamina for an exceptionally athletic Boston terrier dog who was determined to follow her beagle nose and find ways to entertain herself when left to her own devices. Game shows and documentaries were just not her style after being fostered in a home with a six-year-old boy that played endless ball chasing, stick throwing, and imaginary friends hiding in the trees type of games with her. Wes, my husband, would walk her in the park, wrestle with her and join in her zoomie games. This couple loved her as best they could for the two months they had her. But they knew she wasn't happy and Dede was doing her best to show them that. We were asked to take her back. The family knew we loved her and had wanted to add her to our family. The rescue she'd been adopted from (the same rescue Sweetie and pups had been in) had closed. Dede came back to us on July 4th. What a bang! We celebrated with new everything and began integrating her into our family permanently. The lessons she taught Tomas were fast and furious.

He'd be engrossed in his building blocks, and she'd saunter past and steal a block. When she was out of reach, she'd stare at him. It never took long before he'd realize what was going on and give chase. Oh, the hollering and running and stomping of feet. But she taught him so much in that play. Patience or maturity, or both, won, and he learned not to chase, and she eventually stopped stealing his toys. But she still managed to steal his heart. Don't we all have a special place in our hearts for our first love? Through the years, they grew closer.

Maybe it is because he's an only child, or maybe it is because he's homeschooled? They may just have bonded so well because that is what little boys do with their dogs after playing together for endless hours, telling secrets, and sharing the tears of life. Tears of life mean something different when you are raised in a home that rescues.

After Dede's return to our family, we decided to begin our own rescue. For a few years, we mentored with a couple of rescues who taught us a wealth of invaluable information. But nothing can prepare your heart, a child's heart, for rescue. Dede was there for it all. We fostered too many to count; mom dogs with their innumerable pups during Dede's lifetime and each time a new dog walked in the door you could just see it on her face. The rolling eyes and shrug of her shoulder as if to say, "Here we go again." She knew they were broken, battered, or sick.

Dede knew she had work to do in helping them heal. She taught many foster dogs to potty outside or be calm in the crate. Often they just needed reassurance that the tile floors were safe or the TV wasn't going to bite. The mean ceiling fan isn't going to attack and the food bowl will be full again soon. Even stairs can be mountainous if you've never encountered them before. Sometimes she just needed to wear out the obnoxious puppies or gently teach them biting isn't nice. Often a foster dog would only need a snuggle buddy on the soft doggie bed and that was ok too.

Then came the day she was diagnosed with cancer. We had felt the lumps and bumps but told ourselves she's too ornery/tough/young/loved (fill in the blank) to actually have the 'C' word. Three times she underwent the knife in the hopes they could scoop it all out. The veterinarian did a great job of being kind, thorough, informative, and everything you could ask for. It just wasn't enough. After Dede's third surgery and while she was still healing from that, I felt more newly formed lumps. I was incredulous! How could there be new bumps when she still had her cone on and staples in her chest from her previous surgery?

Our family decided quality over quantity was how we would proceed and we didn't think our zoomie-loving Dede would want to spend the rest of her life in a cone undergoing endless surgeries. The cancer took its toll in the following years. But they were quality years of continuing to give her heart to foster dogs needing love, giving love to a growing boy who was beginning his awkward teen years, and the boy struggling with the uncertainty of his daddy leaving for military deployment. Just when I thought the boy and his dog bond couldn't get any stronger, life had to throw a (thankfully uneventful) deployment at us.

Honestly, I eventually learned to joke at adoption events, telling people, "She's never going to die" and "Nobody told her about the 'C' word." I shared her story almost every Saturday for over five years. Five years of her getting frostier in the face and just a little bit more lumpy and bumpy each day. She did start to get slower, and some days she would get a bit crabby. But every day, she asked for belly rubs and waited for Tomas to "accidentally" drop a bit of shredded cheese as he added it to whatever he was cooking that day.

She was always eager to do her "ears" trick. She had those long beagle ears. But she figured out how to make them stand tall like her Boston terrier side of the family can. You just had to laugh.

About the time Dede truly started showing her age and health issues were catching up with her, Lady Anne passed away. We grieved and Lady Anne taught Tomas, and even me, in her own way that this is real. This is happening and no amount of beauty, ornery antics, belly rubs, cheese, or love is going to stop it. I'd powered through an adoption event knowing the horrid conversation with Tomas that needed to happen could not be avoided any longer.

We knew there were no more zoomies, and the ability to comfortably accept hugs or show us "ears" made us certain that to continue her life would only prolong her suffering. Suffering was not ok with Wes, me, and even Tomas knew in his own way, deep inside, that it was time. We gave our tearful filled farewell to her late on that Saturday at the emergency vet clinic.

We still catch ourselves looking for her at unexpected moments. She's not hidden under the pile of blankets on the dog beds or wandering around the yard ignoring my calls to come inside. When it is treat time, Dede isn't shouldering out the others to ensure she gets hers. Tomas has learned that grief comes in waves. Sometimes the grief will hit you with the force to knock your breath away (and maybe bring some unexpected tears), and other times with just a hint of sadness, just enough to maybe coax a hint of a grin because the memory is a sweet one. This grief is new and fresh. Our family is still learning to move on and roll with the waves.

Tomas is almost 18 years old now, and I expect he'll be starting new chapters in his life. New loves, new secrets, and new challenges are in his future. He is sad his future friends will never meet her, and he's sad that his safe secret keeper isn't staring intently, waiting to hear his confession or gaming anecdote or catch a few shreds of dropped cheese. Sometimes it is the things that she did to annoy him while she was able to that are now missed. Her cold nose placed just so under his arm while his gaming buddies are distracting, and he jumps out of his chair. I'm certain she did doggie laughs over that. But I like to think her legacy of teaching dogs and little boys about love and doing zoomies and showing us "ears" was…well, it was everything anyone could ever hope for in a dog's life.

Dede

Maxie, Porter, and Vespa
By Holly Zimmerman

As a child, I can always remember having a pet. We found out at a young age that I was allergic to dog saliva. When I was three years old, my parents got us a kitten. I remember sitting in my parent's station wagon and hearing this tiny, little kitten being run around in circles like she was hopped up on sugar. Her name was Maxie. She was the family pet and my best friend. She was a feisty little thing and wanted attention only on her terms, and she'd bite you when she had enough. My favorite memory of her was when my mom was yelling at one of my brothers for something, and Maxie came up and started to bite her ankles as if she was defending my brothers. How she would tolerate me, I don't have the faintest clue. As a child, I would put bonnets on her or put my scrunchies in her fur to make her "beautiful." Fast forward 18 years, I was 21 when my parents decided it was time to let Maxie go. She lived a long life, but we knew she was sick. I was devastated. I did not know my life without her. I was sad for days. I knew when I was out on my own, I'd get a pet again.

When 2012 came around, my husband (then fiancé) and I bought a house together. We had talked about getting pets. He wanted a dog, and I wanted a cat. Six months after moving in, we found Porter. He was a three-year-old black German

Shepherd mix. He was a big boy weighing in at 86 lbs. The family was looking to rehome him. He was a great dog. He deemed my husband his person. Porter was his boy. Me, well, it took him some training to listen to me. He was so smart and conscious of everything. His bark could scare a village. He was so protective and loyal to us. A little over a year later, we found a kitten named Vespa that we adopted. I immediately fell in love with her, and she became my girl. The shelter was worried about us having Porter and that he may try to prey on her. When we brought Vespa home, we kept them separate and slowly introduced the two. I was amazed at how gentle and aware Porter was of Vespa. Those two became inseparable. They were best buds. You could always see them laying together or Vespa taking over Porter's bed and him just dealing with it and laying on the floor next to her. When they would play together, Porter would be so gentle.

One memory I will never forget is when Vespa got her paw stuck in a door and meowed loudly, and Porter immediately raced over to make sure she was ok. He was worried about his sister, and that melted our hearts. I couldn't believe the relationship those two had. I don't think we will ever see that again with any other pets we have.

When Porter was six, we came home one night from a friend's house and noticed something was weird. The front door had scratches all over the bottom, and there was dried-up saliva on the floor. We had no idea what that was or why Porter would scratch the door because he had never done anything like that before. We found out later that night what had happened. Both my husband and I were awoken to the bed shaking. He thought Porter was just scratching and told him to stop. When the shaking didn't stop, my husband got out of bed and said, "He's having a seizure." My heart dropped, and my stomach churned. Porter had a seizure earlier that night, I realized. The biggest hurt was we were not there for him the first time he had one. His seizure continued for 30 more seconds before he came out of it. He had urinated and expressed his anal glands. He had a grand mal seizure. The look in his eyes broke my heart. He had no idea what was happening. We immediately went to the ER vet. Come to find out, seizures are common in GSDs. There were many options we were given. It could just be a fluke, and he had an imbalance; it could be food, it could be a tumor, or we thought, was there something with the house? We didn't want to dive right in with everything, so we just changed his food and monitored him. Both of us couldn't sleep at night. He would mostly have his seizures at night. When they became more frequent, we knew it wasn't a food allergy. We talked to our vet and then decided to try medication. We ended up having him on the lowest dose of phenobarbital as we have found he is very sensitive to medication despite his size.

We were one month into the medication, and Porter had not had one seizure. My husband had to leave at that point to go on a business trip for three weeks. I was worried about Porter having a seizure while he was gone. Porter had made it through those weeks seizure-free. When my husband came home, it was a sight to see how excited Porter was to have him back. About a week later, Porter ended up having a seizure in the middle of the night. It was really bad, one that lasted for a minute, and he was so disoriented after. He wanted to go outside, and my husband let him out. When Porter walked to the other side of the house, my husband went to guide him back and touched his rear end. That scared him enough that he turned around and bit my husband in the face (we knew it wasn't Porter's fault but ours because we knew not to touch him after a seizure because of the disorientation). Porter did immediately realize who it was and sat down. After an ER trip for the husband, Porter seemed ok for the rest of the day. We went to bed that night exhausted, only to be awoken by Porter having another bad seizure. Once we got everything cleaned up from that and settled back in bed, he had another seizure not even two hours later. It was so bad that after he stopped seizing, he would get up and go to the corner and pant for five minutes. You couldn't call him. It was like he couldn't hear you. When he finally came to, he looked at us with pain in his eyes. We took him to the ER vet, and they said we could run tests and draw blood to see if we could increase his dose of phenobarbital.

Porter hated having his blood drawn, and he was not the same dog after his seizures. I don't understand how for two months, the meds worked, and now they don't. The vet said he could be metabolizing it faster. I don't believe that so much. My thought was he had a tumor. We had a decision to make. We decided to let Porter go as hard as it was. We couldn't be selfish and let him live the rest of his life like this. That was no life for him, and the pain in his eyes after every seizure was enough. We had to send him to the Rainbow Bridge. It was hard. Days after, it didn't feel real. Vespa started to change, and she started urinating in the house, and we couldn't get her to stop. She was grieving for her pal. She looked for him. Meanwhile, in the midst of everything with Porter, we noticed Vespa started to have mini seizures. We took her to the vet, but since it was so infrequent and so minor, there was nothing we could do for it. We really started to think it was something with our house. Was there something in the house that we didn't know about that could have been hurting our pets? We tried to look for any possibility that would explain, but we came up empty-handed. Time had passed, and we had eventually adopted another pup, but the relationship was not the same with Vespa.

In 2017 just after the New Year, my husband and I were watching the *Secret Life of Pets*, and, as usual, Vespa was in my lap cuddling. Little did I know that was the last night I would spend with her. Early in the morning the next day, we were awoken by a large thump. We had no idea what it was, so I got out of bed and found Vespa lying in the hall. I knew something was wrong. She wouldn't get up, and her tail was puffed out. I tried to tickle her back, and she wouldn't move it. I tried to get her to stand, and her back end just flopped. I realized she was paralyzed from the waist down. Within minutes she had defecated and peed all over and was howling in pain. My husband and I knew right then and there what it meant. There was no way she could survive that. We wrapped her up and went to the ER vet yet again. I bawled the whole way there, having to listen to her howl. When we got there, the vet had examined her and came to the conclusion she may have thrown a blood clot, and it was lodged in her artery blocking the area and paralyzing her. She said she could do a blood test that would likely confirm it. As we figured, the results came back that she wasn't getting blood flow to her back end by the lack of blood count there compared to her front end. We asked about our options. Surgery was an option to see and dislodge the clot but for her to regain function was slim. They said she could lead the rest of her life as is but would need a lot of help. She was only three years old. We couldn't let her live like that, so again we had to make that decision not even two years after Porter. We sent Vespa to the Rainbow Bridge to be with her brother. I was broken. I had lost my pal and was depressed for a good six months. Even now, it is hard to recall those times. I don't like to talk about it much.

Even though now we have adopted a dog and a cat again, it will not be the same. I love those two very much, but it is a different kind of love from the first two. I can't give our pets my whole heart now because two pieces of it still belong to Porter and Vespa. Both my husband and I each have memorial tattoos for them, and they both are buried by each other in our yard with their own little gravestone. A cement cat with angel wings for Vespa and an *I love my German Shepherd* steppingstone for Porter.

Vespa and Porter

Carry on My Wayward Daughter
Isabella Rose, Our Angel Girl
By Hope Isabella Lenkersdorf Smith

Dearest Isabella,

Your life's purpose here on earth was to save our little family. You entered your new forever family while we were in our darkest hours. You came to us out of your own free will and gave us the rest of your far too short life. It was a life cut short, not by you, nature, or even God.

You arrived in our front garden three months before our boy. Now your brother crossed over to the Rainbow Bridge. We first encountered you while you were lying in one of the planters for the potted palm trees when we heard your meows through the screen of the open dining room window. At first, you were hard to distinguish from the soil at the base of the plant, but then you opened your beautiful green eyes for us to see. You stretched and yawned and playfully chased the geckos that were hiding in the plants. At this point, you were simply irresistible, so we came out to meet and greet you. From then on, we began keeping you on the lanai at night to keep you safe from other Florida predators.

It was your warm open heart with just the right amount of feline spunk and individualism that attracted us to you. From nearly the moment we first met you, we knew you would be part of our family.

All during SoCrates last month's here on earth, you watched over all of us, protecting us and giving your complete and unconditional love and devotion. Every morning at exactly 9:00 a.m. you would call out to your new daddy telling him it was time to rise and shine and that you were ready for your breakfast.

Daddy had always let you into the house on those mornings for a private play date for just the two of you. Daddy let you explore your new home and you managed to wiggle your way into every space and cubby hole no matter how small. We are still so very sorry that we could not let you stay inside with us full time. You now knew Isabella and I believe that you knew even then as to why. SoCrates was so very sick and if he would have seen you, he would have so very much wanted to play with you, his new sister. He possibly would have gotten over-excited and even possibly hurt himself. At this point in his life, SoCrates did not have much energy left so we needed to be extremely careful with his energy expenditures.

During the two months after SoCrates had passed Mommy, Daddy and Lily had all been suffering greatly and were completely heartbroken. Isabella, you did the funniest things each day amusing us greatly, this allowed us to laugh and smile at your goofball antics. Little by little each day, you, our baby girl Isabella helped our hearts to heal and even feel the tiniest glimmer of happiness again. Isabella, you saved our family from complete despair.

Two months and two days after our golden son SoCrates crossed over to the Rainbow Bridge, Jesus also called you home. Your life's mission on earth was now complete. Thus, being so, Jesus wanted you to receive your reward of eternal life with your brother SoCrates, the brother you were always meant to have and forever be with.

Even though we had lost two of our three fur babies within two months of each other, my heart is still so very happy because I know that our golden son SoCrates and you, our feline daughter, Isabella, spend your days playing together. You guys can play with the rest of your packs and your fur families at the Rainbow Bridge.

Even though I know that you two precious souls have crossed over to the Rainbow Bridge, I know that you still come home to sleep with us every night.

Isabella Rose Smith
August 13th, 2016 – you were born
June 12th, 2018 – you crossed over the Rainbow Bridge

We love you, Isabella.
We miss you, Isabella.
You will forever be our daughter, our Isabella Rose.

Isabella Rose

Sweet Child of Mine
SoCrates Kan
Hope Isabella Lenkersdorf Smith

There are truly thousands of stories that I could tell about you, SoCrates, as every minute of your life on earth with us as our son is a story in it and of itself.

On a particularly sad day for me since you crossed over the Rainbow Bridge, I was outside in our front yard thinking about which story I was going to tell about you for this book; the memory came to mind of the time grandma was driving you and me to the park for a play date with your packmates. I believe that this is the story that you want me to tell about you. This story truly shows just how smart you were and how you knew exactly what had happened.

G-ma was taking you and me to the park that night because Daddy had to go to work and needed the car. On these nights it would fall to your G-ma to play the role of chauffeur. She spent many a night at the park with us as she always enjoyed your play dates with your pack. G-ma loved you very, very much, and ever since she moved to Florida, she would spend every second possible with us and your friends when she came back to New York to visit.

As per normal on these nights, when G-ma would drive you hopped into the back seat of her car and took your usual spot smack dab in the middle of the back seat. This was just one more reason why your grandma used to call you Sheldon.

I had just put you in the car and at the last second realized that I had forgotten to bring the Milk-Bones. You and your packmates loved to snack on Milk-Bones as you guys ran amuck in the park. The snacks would help keep up everyone's energy as you guys often played for several hours at a time.

I had closed the car door and proceeded to walk up the front steps of the house when I turned back to see you and G-ma driving away. My first thought to myself was that she was going to be in for a big surprise when she gets to the park and realizes I'm not in the car with you guys. I could only guess that she didn't hear me when I told her I had forgotten the Milk-Bones and to wait.

I tried to call her on her cell phone, but as usual, it was not turned on. G-ma had always said that her cell phone was for her use when she needed it while she was away from home. It was not for receiving unwanted calls from strangers trying to sell her bundled cable packages. However, I am sure that this was one phone call that she would have been happy to get.

I quickly ran into the house and told Daddy what had taken place, so he got ready for work early and rushed me to the park so I could rescue you from G-ma's attempted dog napping. Daddy and I got to the park at about the same time G-ma was parking her car. Fortunately for us, we were able to take the parking spot directly behind her. When G-ma got out of her cart and saw Daddy and me get out of our car, the look of confusion on her face was hysterical and priceless. Right now as I write this I am seeing the whole scene play out in my head and laughing out loud. This was truly a hysterical moment for all of us.

When G-ma looked in the back of her car and saw you sitting there all by yourself, she couldn't help but begin to laugh. You were sitting there in true golden retriever style all regal and majestic, wearing the biggest smile you ever had from floppy ear to floppy ear. Your huge smile made G-ma laugh so hard that tears began streaming down her face and she began to have trouble catching her breath. I am sure that to passersby all three of us must have looked like we were insane because of our uncontrollable laughter. I'm sure that they were wondering what was so funny.

I finally composed myself enough to open the back door of her car and let you out, but then I saw the look in your eyes and the tremendous smile on your face. You had the look of complete understanding in your eyes of what had just taken place. My heart skipped a beat and a real tear of joy began flooding down my cheek. I always knew how intelligent you were and your smile made it clear how funny you thought this whole situation was. Many people simply don't understand how smart dogs can be; golden retrievers as a breed in general and you in particular. In your eyes, I saw that you knew how much you were loved by us and how much that we loved you.

While you were playing with your friends in the park, G-ma and I were telling your packmates' parents the story of what had happened during the ride to the park. G-ma said that she had been talking to me all the while during the trip. She could not tell that I wasn't in the car as your big head took up the whole rearview mirror since you were sitting directly in the middle of the rear seat. She was telling the other parents that while she drove, she could see you smiling all the way to the park like you were in on some kind of secret joke. All along, she was wondering why I hadn't answered her. When we all got to the park, and G-ma realized that I wasn't in the car with you guys, she finally got your joke, SoCrates.

Just as I was writing the last sentence of your previous story SoCrates, another memory of you at the park came to mind. Just as with the earlier story I believe that you want me to tell this one also. It is yet another example of your wit and wonderful sense of humor.

It was a cold January and the entire New York area had just been hit by a major snowstorm. A significant amount of snow fell in a twenty-four-hour period with drifts in many cases exceeding six feet. I had tried walking you in our neighborhood up and down many blocks but could not get very far with all of the huge snow drifts. The snow on the sidewalks was easily up to my hip, which meant it was well past your head. With all of the snow, you had not gone to the bathroom for more than two days, so Daddy and I both knew what had to be done.

You had always been a stinker and very particular about where you went potty. Daddy and I both knew that the only solution to solve your bathroom dilemma was a trip down to Howard Beach Park.

Daddy and I put you in our Tahoe, put the truck in four-wheel drive, and off to the park we went driving through the aftermath of a hellacious snowstorm. Then in order to make any progress towards the park, Daddy had to drive up and down one-way streets the wrong way because they were the only ones plowed for emergency vehicles to get through the neighborhood – and for us, especially you, this was an emergency.

Driving to the park usually took less than ten minutes, but on this day, it took at least half an hour. Through it all, Daddy got us to the park. Once we were there, your father had to drive on the footpath to get us even close to the field where you usually play and do your business. You and I got out of the car while Daddy stayed, just in case we got stuck in the snow and he had to come and rescue us.

As always you were delighted with all of the snow and took off running as best that you could. Being a golden retriever, you had short legs, but you were unbelievably strong, so off through the mounds of newly fallen snow you went.

From a distance, in the very middle of the field, there seemed to be a huge snowman that someone had made earlier in the storm. I was closer to the car near Daddy, but you saw it and took off like a bat out of hell running for it. As I followed behind you as best I could through the deep snow, I began to see the figure more clearly and that it was not a snowman at all, actually it was very far from a snowman, not even close. Someone, probably a group of teenagers, had made a giant snow penis. It stood at least six feet tall – balls included. Once I had realized what it was, I simply fell over laughing in the snow.

As fast as I could, I started digging through the recesses of the pockets of my bulky snow suit to try and find my cell phone to take a picture of this magnificent work of art. However, by the time I found my phone you had circled the snow penis and began to lift your leg to take a leak on it. Miraculously in the nick of time, I got the perfect picture. I wish I had taken a video of this precious moment, but it happened so fast that I am lucky to have gotten the shot that I did.

Once I had gotten the picture, I fell onto my knees laughing so hard that my side began to hurt. SoCrates, you saw me sitting in the snow and made your way over to me. You seemed to be very proud and pleased with yourself for what you had just done. I thank you for making me laugh uncontrollably with delight. Daddy saw us both rolling in the snow, so he got out of the car and joined us as fast as he could to join in on the fun in the snow.

SoCrates, Daddy, and me rolling in the fresh deep snow that clear, cold, and quiet night, just the three of us, is what my heaven is and what I hope it will be when the day comes that we are all reunited together forever. Now, of course, with the addition of Lily and Isabella.

SoCrates, you changed Daddy and me forever. I am not the same person that I was before you came into our lives. Daddy and I thank God and you for this every day of our lives.

I thank God for the blessing of you as our son. Daddy always tells you that you changed the world.
You did SoCrates.

SoCrates Kan Smith
November 8th, 2005 – born in Budapest
April 10th, 2018 – you crossed over the Rainbow Bridge in Bradenton, Florida.

You are reunited with all of your packmates, your golden fur parents, and all of your brothers and sisters. You will forever be our golden son, Boo Bear.

SoCrates Kan

It Happens Every Time
By Jayne Malone

I have loved dogs my whole life. When I get a new puppy and see the look in their little eyes it's always love at first sight. It was like that with Brandy. It happens every time. She was one of the smartest dogs I have had, a black mini schnauzer. She was a handful at first when I brought her home. I set up a huge crate for her to sleep in. She didn't like it at all, she cried for a week. I wouldn't give in and either would she. She eventually got the idea that the crate was her own little bedroom and learned to go in it at bedtime.

Brandy loved to bark at anything; it was one of her bad habits. She also loved to play and run. I got Teekee when Brandy was five years old, and they became friends right away. Brandy even let Teekee share her bedroom crate. Teekee never liked to play much, so Brandy played fetch with me most of the time.

Then when Teekee turned five, I got Day-z. It was love at first sight for Brandy and Day-z. Brandy was getting older but tried her best to play with Day-z. As the years went on, Brandy got a rare eye disease. Her eyes looked normal, but she went blind very suddenly. Day-z never left her side and became Brandy's seeing eye dog.

Then I found out Brandy had cancer. It was one of the worst days of my life, and hers. She did okay for about a year, but then the cancer spread to her brain. She would try and walk then she would collapse. I had to carry her in and out to go potty. Day-z would lay next to her as close as she could to make Brandy feel safe.

Then the day came…that day we all know will come. The night before Brandy couldn't walk, she ate her dinner and drank some water. She was next to me on the sofa, just staring as if she saw something. I thought to myself she must be seeing heaven. Then I thought she isn't the happy, playful Brandy I knew anymore. There was nothing left of her. The night before I took her in to say goodbye, I was very calm. That surprised me. But maybe because I knew I was doing what was best for her, and that's why I was so at peace. The next morning poor Brandy tried to eat. The food fell out of her mouth; she collapsed next to the food dish. Poor Day-z sat faithfully next to Brandy. The sad look on her face broke my heart. The calmness from the night before was gone. I took one of Brandy's favorite soft blankets with me. When I got to my vet's office, I told him I had to let her go, he said she was half gone already. I placed the soft blanket on the exam table. The vet gave her the first shot, and I spent what seemed like hours saying goodbye to her. Then the final shot was given. A look of peace came onto her face. I knew I did the right thing. Brandy was 16 years old. I gave her the best life I could, Brandy was loved and spoiled her whole life.

It doesn't make it any easier, but we all know this happens every time. Every time we love a dog. But despite knowing what is coming in the end, we give our love. Every time.

Teekee, Brandy, Day-z

The Smallest Puppy
By Jennifer Norman

His story began on a warm day in April. I was handed the smallest puppy I had ever seen. I'd never taken in a puppy that young and small. At only five weeks old the puppies' mom had stopped feeding them so homes had to be found. He was a pit bull pup, a tiny black pit bull pup; not the most popular color or breed so of course, my first thought was, *sign me up.* I named this tiny bundle of energy Jacoby Joseph. He joined a pack of a Husky named, Mia, and a Boxer named, Jackson.

He was so small that I carried him everywhere. I was so afraid of Parvo that I never let his feet touch the ground outside of his crate. I realize this seems excessive, but he was too small at that time to get the vaccine. He used potty pads inside and was usually perched atop my shoulder or being carried like a baby. This continued into his adulthood. Until carrying an 80-pound dog like a baby became difficult.

I soon learned that this adorable pup had some issues, some very concerning issues. Most of the time Jacoby was a normal puppy but sometimes he seemed, well, crazy. Mentally unstable. Completely out of his mind. Not vicious or anything just mental. The vet diagnosed him with OCD. He would find an object, focus on it and not let it go. It could be a brick, a piece of wood, his leash, anything. His biggest trigger was hearing a dog that he couldn't see. Unfortunately for us, we had a fence and another dog lived on the other side of it. Now, when I say he wouldn't let it go, I mean literally. He went into a zone where he would pant, whine, and hold onto whatever he was fixated on and would do nothing else. If I tried to remove said object, well, I got bit. Now when he was tiny, it wasn't that bad, but as he grew so did his teeth. If I didn't remove it from his sight, he would not come out of his OCD fit.

I also discovered that he was fearless, and not in a good way. He had no fear for his own self-preservation. He'd have run into a burning building out of sheer curiosity. If I dropped something and it was loud all the other dogs ran away from it, he ran towards it.

Don't get me wrong, he was a sweet puppy, a normal puppy most of the time. He played with the other dogs and snuggled with me on the couch when it was naptime. Ninety-nine percent of the time he was a totally normal guy. Now I knew these instances of OCD would need to be addressed before he grew up so I consulted vets, trainers, and anyone I thought could help us. We took so many obedience classes that he perfectly behaved anytime we were out and was easy to control. But those freakouts, as I started to call them, those freakouts were when all the training meant nothing. He simply did not hear me saying the words. It was the oddest thing. He only ever did this at home and I was the only person he ever bit.

What has to be understood is that this wasn't his fault. It wasn't my fault. It just was. Nothing was done to him to make him this way, he was born with these issues and I never blamed him for anything he did. I didn't get mad at him. Frustrated, yes, but never mad. It did get old having to go get a finger or my hand sewn up from the bites. As he grew, so did his strength and teeth.

A lot of people told me I should get rid of him. Give him away. That was never an option. Why in the world would I give my sweet boy to someone who didn't understand him? That wouldn't keep him safe? I spent a small fortune on trainers and vets, medications and books on training dogs with issues.

One of my favorite stories of Jacoby is when we were driving quite a long way to see a different trainer. He had a special seat belt harness that kept him safe when we were driving, however, the seatbelt had to be fastened for it to keep him put. Well, he figured out how to unlock his seatbelt. So, I pulled over and fastened it back. I started driving again and he unlocked it again. Only this time he also unlocked mine too and looked at me as if to say, "Freedom is yours, Mom!" I was laughing so hard. He was always a character for sure. Of course, when we got to the facility he behaved perfectly, and the trainer didn't understand why we were there. I had taken a video of one of his freakouts and showed it to her. She was at a loss. She'd never seen anything like that before. She had no solution for us. The $300 an hour trainer said she couldn't help us. Another dead end, more disappointment, and Jacoby kept getting bigger and stronger every day.

Fast forward two and a half years later. Jacoby is an 80-pound beautiful American pit bull terrier. He was striking to look at. A perfect specimen. I had him neutered of course, as soon as it was possible. So, all the breeding requests were met with aggravation and disdain. I rescue dogs, not breed them. He's still a good boy 99% of the time and he still has his freakouts. They come in spurts at this point. Clusters in a way. We could go months without one and then suddenly he'd get triggered and then we'd have several in a few days. Those were the bad times. Those days were horrible. By now, Mia had gone to the Bridge and we'd added a female AmStaff named Bella and a female American bulldog named Jasmine. Both bred almost to death. Jacoby did well with the other dogs, though he never really got to meet Jasmine.

We'd just added her to the pack when *it* happened. One of the worst days of my life, and I've had some pretty bad ones, but this day. I'd give anything to have it back to do differently.

It was a Sunday in October. A beautiful day. We'd just gotten up and around. I'd let everyone out to go to the bathroom and fed everyone when my worst nightmare came true. Jacoby had a freakout in the house, and the object of his OCD was, of all things, me. The vet had warned me this could happen, but I didn't think it ever would. Now there's no way for me to remove myself from him. And so, like any object of his OCD, part of me ended up in his mouth being shaken like a rag doll. It's important to note here that I never got mad at him. I just kept saying, "Oh baby, what have you done?" I knew we'd crossed a line that couldn't be uncrossed. Biting me when I'm trying to take something away from him to end a freakout is one thing; biting me because I am the something, that's completely different. I don't want to go into detail but suffice it to say that I was very injured, and he wasn't stopping.

It wasn't an attack, just a grab and let go unless I tried to move away, then he grabbed again. I finally made it to my bedroom and shut the door. My options here were few. I couldn't allow a friend to come in; he might hurt them. I had to go because I needed stitches. So, I did the most horrible thing. I called AC. I managed to slip out the front door, and they came and got him out of the house. I wanted to die. None of this was his fault, none of it. After he was taken out, I went to the hospital and pretty much cried all the rest of the day. Rehashing in my head how I could have done something different. The next day I went up to AC to ask them to give him his medicine and let me see him. They wouldn't do either. But I was told he could do his bite hold at our vet's office if they approved it, which my vet did. They moved him to the vet's office for boarding, and I went to see my baby and make sure he got his medicine. Now, I know some will judge me for calling AC to begin with, but I genuinely couldn't think of another option. I couldn't safely allow a friend or family member to attempt to crate him in the house.

Back to the vet's office. I went to see him every day, he had to stay there for 10 days. I even went on the weekends because one of the techs was a friend and she let me go up there with her.

At this point, I had every intention of bringing my baby home. Not even a second thought about it. Everyone was telling me that I was insane for wanting to bring him back home. I had to have a lot of stitches to sew my arm back together and I had a couple of other injuries. But they didn't understand. It was never his fault. I loved my dog, unconditionally, no matter what he did to me. It wasn't because he wanted to do it, he had a mental disease. I made an appointment with a trainer in another state for a couple of days after he got out.

He was there for 10 days and gained about 10 pounds because I took him treats every day. On the last evening, before he could come home, something happened that had never happened before. He had a freak out somewhere other than home and he almost bit someone other than me. Unbeknownst to me, someone had put a female in estrus in a pen while we were outside in the yard playing. He lost his mind and had one of the worst freakouts he had ever had. One of the techs came running back and even though I told her to get out of there and let me get him put up, she insisted on doing her job. He almost bit her. More than once. We got him put in his pen and I tried to calm him down but it wasn't happening. He needed time and they were closing.

Still, at that moment I intended to bring my baby home. But I had a lot of thinking to do. What kind of life would he have, never going anywhere anymore for fear of a public freakout? Me always worried if he'd fixate on me or one of the other dogs. It was a long agonizing night. I decided to talk to our vet, a man I admired and respected. He had taken care of all my dogs and saved many of my very sick rescues. We had a very good relationship. We did until he retired, now his daughter is our vet. I called him and we talked about Jacoby's options. He said he really didn't feel it would be safe for me to bring him home and that I had given Jacoby the best life he could have had, given him more love than anyone ever would have, but it was time to give him peace.

I had to agree. Because I loved him, I had to let them kill him. It's horrible to put it that way but that's just what it was. I went to the vet's office after work and held him as they gave him the peace he deserved. There wasn't a dry eye in the room. I loved him, the techs loved him, and the vet even cried. It was the right thing to do but it destroyed me. I had failed him. I live with it every day. A part of me died with Jacoby, a part I've never gotten back, don't know that I ever will.

A few days after, I spoke to the woman I got Jacoby from. Her brother was the guy that owned Jacoby's parents. She had taken Jacoby's sister. Her name was Rosy. I found out that Rosy had been put down after attacking the lady's husband. The brother had been inbreeding these dogs to make them look perfect. The whole litter was dead. Every puppy born with my baby was already dead because they were all mentally unstable. Jacoby had lived the longest. I begged her to tell me where to find her brother, but she would not. That's probably for the best.

This is Jacoby's story. He deserves to have it told. My sweet baby. The smallest puppy I had ever seen.

Jacoby

Heidl
By Jonell Pope

Death is such a hard and permanent thing to deal with. We mourn the loss of a pet the same way we mourn the loss of a friend or a family member. My pain has been tripled not only by the loss of my Heidl on December 17th, 2018, but not even a month later the passing of my brother's dog Dixie, who we were very close with. But then to be amplified even more by the death of my brother the following month on February 11th. I feel like I have not had time to grieve properly because of the swift loss of so many close to me. I think that is why Heidl's passing has hit me so, so hard and feels like it was just last week that she passed away. I grieve for all. I have decided to write this letter to my Heidl in hopes of letting some of the pain out. I also will be writing a letter to my brother to help with the pain of his leaving. Writing these two letters will be very difficult; however, let me first preface with a little background history.

Someone had once suggested that we share our memorial for our fur babies that have passed on. They said it might help with our grief. I do not know if that is true, but I am going to do that anyway. I am hoping that by writing a letter it will help me to cope. I know that we cannot keep it in us; it has to be let out to eventually heal and move on with my life.

I have had at least 12 dogs and cats in my life that have passed on to the Rainbow Bridge. These do not include the ones from close family members that have been part of our extended family. None of them have been easy; none of them get any easier to handle.

I lost my Heidl on December 17th, 2018, one week before Christmas. I used to cry every day, but now not so often, but I miss her every day. I found a music box that I had gotten for a previous dog that says *Forever with the Angels* – it hits me very hard. Sad to say, this is a permanent thing. We will never see them again until we pass on and meet them on the Rainbow Bridge, then together to everlasting life. I read somewhere our pets come into our lives to make us happy and when their work is done, they leave us.

I know it's hard, but we need to move on with our lives. Some of us have other pets that rely on us and love us. Our special babies will never be replaced but we have a life to live and we must live it.

Heidl was my favorite, but most people do not understand our connection. I had her for 14 of her 15.5 years. Just take your time and someday you will find peace and hopefully another fur baby that you can share your life with. Prayers and hugs for all of you.

My dear beloved Heidl,
First of all, Sweetie, I want to say I still miss you terribly, but you already know that don't you? Not a day goes by that I do not think of you. You were so special to me; you were always my defender and protector. I turn on your flameless candle by your memorial every morning and shut it off every night. I give you a kiss every day, but you never give me kisses back anymore.

I am sad and it will take a long while if ever, to get over you. I would prefer to remember the good times in this letter, just to remind you of them and especially me.

You do not know this, but you almost came to visit with us before your previous owner passed on. We had a hurricane coming, and he lived on the beach, but he had to evacuate and could not take you with him. This gentleman's daughter knew Uncle Jeff, and since we lived on the mainland and had had many Keeshonden before, they decided I might be able to provide you with a safe haven to ride out the storm. As it turned out, your previous owner decided not to leave the beach, so you did not come to visit us. Many months went by, and your previous owner passed away. I will never forget when I got the call from Uncle Jeff telling me you had been surrendered and homeless and that I could go and see you at the SPCA. He told me your name was Heidi, and it seemed to be fate that I should have you as our first keeshond's name was Heidi also.

I sent Gary to check on you first; he said you were a chubby dog but seemed quite nice and friendly. I decided I had to go and meet you also. Unknown to me, you would be coming home with me that day as you were willed to us. I called Daddy on my way home and told him we had a new dog. She was an overweight Keeshond named Heidi. We both fell in love with you, and you fit into our family very well. You never tried to run away. You knew you were *home.* We decided that we could not have another dog named Heidi as it would be too confusing. We thought hard about what to call you, and Daddy suggested "Heidl." We figured you would just think we had an accent or lisp. You adjusted almost immediately to the name, and we were all happy.

You were always my protector; you enjoyed jumping up on the bed and lying right on my chest. You almost took my breath away, but you never stayed there too long. We just had to meet heart to heart and then sleep in our separate spaces. You used to jump on the bed in the morning and lie on my chest as Daddy left for work and growl at him as to say, "She's mine and I will protect her!"

Through the years we all grew as a family and had multiple dogs come and go through our family. We did go on trips, but I wish we would have gone more. At times we had up to four dogs, but it was quite difficult to travel with all of you. Oftentimes, you got left behind with another sibling because it was too hot for you. I wish you had been able to experience more trips. I wish a lot for you, but you are gone now.

The things I love and remember:

I used to close the back door to keep you and your brother and sister outside to finish your "business," but when you were ready to come in you always used to sit at the back door and bark to remind me you were ready to come back in. Woof, woof!

You had the most identifiable run just like a bunny rabbit; two back legs then two front legs – you definitely had a hop. I loved your puffy bunny tail; a tightly coiled cotton ball tail. I loved the way you used to wiggle it. Nothing else would wiggle, just the puff and you would grin at me when I ruffled it.

You used to love to lay on your back, showing your full furry belly, and legs widespread. It was as if you were asking for a belly rub, which you usually got. I always loved the way you laid on your chest and crossed your front paws. Our little Miss Prissy was watching and attentive to everything going on; you would look at me with those deep brown puppy dog eyes, and you had me wrapped around your paw.

When you first came to us you used to nip at my ankles every time I walked to the door. I think you were telling me, "Please don't go!" You never hurt me but you got my attention.

Let me remind you of your rubber balls. You used to carry around the squeaky ball. We called it your "baby ball" because we decided you thought it was your baby. You always had a couple of them, and if you had one, we would grab the other one and squeak it. Then you would drop the first one and come get the second one. Then we would get the first one again, and that made you mad, and you would then put both in your mouth and walk away. You would then lie down and keep them close to protect them.

Anytime I was working on my office computer, you decided it was either lunchtime or you just wanted my attention by nudging my arm. I would pet you and pat you on the head; you were then content to go lie back down and wait.

You used to rub your back on the pool table and moan in joy. It was that area that felt so good to be scratched and we could not scratch it all the time and you could not reach it either. I would then go over to you and scratch your back for you and you would continue with your moaning in joy.

You were a healthy dog most of your life. I will never forget when I took you to the vet and they said you had elevated liver enzymes and it might be cancer. I was not ready to lose you yet and I took off work to go get a specialist opinion and an ultrasound. I was never so happy to find out it was not cancer, just an elevation, and I had to watch those levels for the rest of your life. I feel I was given extra borrowed time with you. You were always able to hold your own and loved your special diet and food – which came after one of your vet visits told me you were overweight and needed to lose some weight. I went home and searched "overweight keeshond" and your picture popped up. Oh my, you were not a keeshond but a Norwegian elkhound. Even when I told the vet, he agreed with me and never told me you needed to lose weight again.

When you became so sick in the end, I felt it was your liver, but we did not put you through any invasive testing, not at your age. You had a good life and we decided to just keep you happy and comfortable. I had to get up with you at night to take you outside because you were too weak to get up on your own. I went through so many different foods just to try to keep you eating healthy. For some, you turned your nose up from the very beginning. I threw away so much food just to try to get you to eat. After a while I decided to give the food you would not eat to your brother and sister. They loved it, but they gained weight (after you were gone, they lost the weight but missed the extra rich food). We tried many different medications to help with your appetite but in the end, you gave up. Remember when I made you the filet mignon for dinner with a baked potato? Daddy was so jealous, but you ate it like it was last your meal, which I thought it was but the next morning you were up and chipper again. I even made you your favorite cheese grits and you eventually even turned them down. That was when I knew it was time to let you go. I tried to make our final goodbye something special for both of us. We went on a car ride just the two of us to Burger King and I got you a hamburger, fries, and ice cream in a cup. We then went to the park and sat on the grass in the sun by the lake. We had the best quality time. I had a chance to take many last pictures of you just enjoying yourself along with me. You loved the hamburger but spit out the pickles. You ate most of the fries also, but I guess you were too full for the ice cream. I took a video of you eating your final meal and I still cry when I watch it. We then took our last ride together to the vet's office, they were all so nice and considerate. They made you and me comfortable while we rested quietly together on the floor. You then just drifted off to sleep; I hope you know I was close by you till the very end and beyond. It was such an empty feeling driving home alone. When I got home, your brother and sister kept sniffing me and looking around for you. I just cried in their fur, then Bailey gave me his squeaky toy and made me smile.

Your brother and sister missed you when I got home. Bailey especially comforted me. Brie is not doing well now; I feel she will be joining you soon. You and Dixie keep an eye out for her. I hope you and Dixie are keeping Uncle Jeff company and playing nicely with the balls. Did Dixie teach you to catch a frisbee yet?

I love you always,
Mom

If there ever comes a day when we cannot be together, put me in your heart, I will stay there forever. – A.A. Milne

Heidl

Meant To Be
By Kaitlin Yoder

A 15-year-old girl walked by a litter of puppies for sale at a flea market in the early, chilly morning of November 2009. There was a black and tan puppy, so small she could fit in just a hand. She shivered, alone. Like any young girl would do when spotting a sorrowful-looking, large-eye-baring puppy, she begged her dad to let her buy the lonely dog. The girl's dad called to talk to her mom and asked if they should bring a puppy home.

"We already have a dog," they both responded.

The mom then said, "If she is there at the end of the day, she's meant to be."

Reluctantly, the girl went throughout the day with her heart and mind longing for that small puppy, huddled into a little ball in the corner of her cage on the ground.

At the end of the day, she raced to the kennel and was delighted to see the puppy was still there. As if still tempting fate, the girl had to get through one more obstacle though; one more to call this puppy hers. The couple selling her wanted $100 for her. Her dad said she could only buy the puppy if the couple would sell her for $50. Much to the father's surprise, a happy little girl came trotting back with a small puppy in her hands.

That was the day that 15-year-old girl found her best friend and hugged her all the way home.

I'm Kaitlin, and that small black and tan puppy was a chorkie pup named Pipi. This is where our story began.

Pipi's beginning of life wasn't as easy and perfect as I wish it would have been. For such a special soul, she deserved all the world. The very first day we brought her home, and she was no bigger than my mother's hand, my brother stepped on her. We weren't used to having such a small dog around. We had grown up with big dogs like German Shepherds, Rottweilers, and Mastiffs. It was a change for all of us.

I was so filled with excitement to have a new puppy home. My mother shared a deep connection with Pipi too. She spent all her mornings and evenings with that girl, but my mom worked many hours. Often, Pipi would spend her days alone in the beginning. I was navigating the heart of my teenage years, and although I loved Pipi too, I was spending nights at football games, volleyball tournaments, youth groups, and sleepovers.

As Pipi got a bit older, she was allowed to spend more time outside of her crate. She became best friends with our other dog, a miniature pincher named Dexter. They ran around in circles together, slept in bed together, ate together, played together, and spent every minute together. Dexter became her whole world.

I grew older, and so did Pipi. We spent many nights together, sobbing over lost boyfriends and teenage turmoil. She watched boys and friends come and go, my first car, and the stresses of high school and graduation. She spent many nights with me as we processed the deep pain of a broken family and navigated what life with divorced parents looked like for me. Eventually, I moved out and went to college, leaving my girl behind. It still breaks my heart to think I missed a whole year of her life.

One day, I received a phone call in June from my mother. Pipi and Dexter had been poisoned. She was only able to take Pipi to the emergency vet. Pipi was failing and her health was very fragile. After almost a month in the pet hospital, Pipi made it out of the hospital and came home with me. I had finally moved into a home just two months before Pipi's poisoning where I was allowed to have dogs. My mom and I spent many days nursing Pipi back to full health at our home. We still don't know how she was poisoned and what really happened. Throughout this time, I bonded hard with my best friend and became closer to her than I had ever been. Pipi had found her happy forever home with me.

Years went by and my time revolved around her. My fiancée and I lived together and she was our whole world. Everything we did revolved around what we could do with her. Is this restaurant dog friendly? Are these trails dog friendly? Will this friend allow a dog to come to their home? Make sure to pack her day bag. Make sure to pack her night bag. Make sure to pack her hiking bag. Will she be able to sleep if she isn't in her bed? Can't go on vacation if she can't come. So many thoughts like these filled our daily lives.

The second summer she lived with us, we spent every weekend for six months exploring all the state parks around us. We went to almost every state park in Iowa and explored other states together as well. Pipi was an outdoor girl. She loved spending time outside and going on hikes. She was the perfect dog for me, being everything I needed her to be. My shotgun rider, my ride or die, my hiking partner, my companion.

That's when we were happiest, on a hike and in the car. Pipi had never had any sort of proper training but she was the smartest dog I had ever met. I know, I know. It's like having a kid – your kid is always the best, right? We definitely had kid syndrome. We were so proud of her. She was so intelligent, gentle, and kind. She would bark in excitement and run to the door when asked if she was ready to go on a hike. We would harness her up, grab her hiking leash, pack a backpack with lunch for her and us, hook her water bowl to our backpack and away we would go. She would sit on my lap, watching out the window in excitement for our next stop. We would spend the days hiking around state parks and that little 12-pound chorkie would do absolutely anything asked of her. She never acted tired, never stopped, always wanted to be near us. She would wade through streams, run up as many stairs as needed, sit in a backpack when the stairs got to be too much or the trail became too bumpy.

She was just as good off-leash as she was on-leash. Not a worry ever crossed my mind that she would run away. She kept on our heels and never steered too far. She knew she was loved by us, she knew she would find adventure with us, and she never took that for granted. There was nothing more peaceful than after a long day of hiking watching Pipi sleep in the back, country music playing quietly on the radio, the sun setting, and the road winding ahead of us.

Our girl felt more human than dog most days. She slept in between my husband and me, head on my pillow and blanket covering her body. If the evening got too late and we still hadn't gone to bed yet, she would heave a heavy sigh, walk to the bed and tuck herself in with her head on a pillow and her body under a blanket. She was a girl of habit, and if she wasn't able to sleep in her king-sized, memory foam bed with both her parents on either side of her, she didn't sleep. When we traveled or stayed at a friend's house with her, she didn't sleep. If one of us was gone that night, she didn't sleep. When my mom would stay at our house to watch her when we traveled, Pipi would go to her bed and tuck herself in and try to sleep. She would not sleep with my mom. We laughed about what a princess she was.

She preferred ice in her water, did not like dog treats, preferred deli meat, chicken, or grilled steak, did not care for other dogs much at all, loved when people would pay attention to her, had a favorite toy shaped like a doughnut, did not understand the game of fetch but instead loved the game of chase and loved getting dirty swimming in ponds and streams, but gave big puppy dog eyes of sadness when it came time for a bath. She knew just what she liked in her short years of life.

Not only did Pipi get to witness the heart of my teenage years, but she also walked into young adulthood with me. She watched an engagement, participated in our wedding, lived in our first home with us, stayed up with me at night while I worked on college assignments, and even got to spend days with me at my first adult job. I had graduated from college and began a career in geriatric social work. Since Pipi was so well behaved and enjoyed the company of people so much she would make her rounds with me at work some days. When I became the head of my department, Pipi came to work with me every day.

The residents enjoyed watching her puppy streaks come out again. She would put on a show and throw treats in the air, chase toys around that they would throw, and cuddle up in their laps after a rousing game of chase. Often, I would leave her in their laps and let her snooze peacefully as I continued the rest of my day. Eventually, she would come trotting back into my office when she was ready for a snack. She knew her way around the nursing home just as well as any human, and she would make rounds on her own.

She created a sense of connection in some of the residents as well. As Pipi aged with the residents, her ailments tended to be very similar to the resident's ailments. Arthritis began to creep in, and her body moved a little slower. Her heart started to show signs of congestive heart failure, her muzzle greyed, and her eyes dimmed just slightly. She began to take pills like what many of the residents were taking. She became a sense of connection for the residents; someone else was going through this too. They would pet her and ask her questions about how she was feeling while explaining what they were feeling. She was their release, if only briefly.

In the last year of her life, I spent every hour with Pipi. She came to work with me daily, to friends' houses, and into stores in a bag or a stroller. People never saw one of us without the other and would expect us to come, often making sure treats were always available in the store or home. We were literally never apart.

Around eight years old, Pipi began to cough some. I didn't notice it at first but decided to take her to the vet. After X-rays and a checkup, the vets discovered Pipi had a heart valve disorder. The blood wasn't pumping through the heart correctly.

My whole world crashed. My best friend, my baby, my soul was sick, and there was nothing I could do to stop or treat it.

She was put on an extensive list of medications. I was desperate. I searched the internet high and low for any sort of relief or treatment. I bought any supplement I could get my hands on. I changed her diet to the most highly recommended and expensive diet I could find. I literally could not imagine a world without her in it. I couldn't think about her not waiting by the shower until I got out, not snoring on the edge of the bed as I worked, not hearing her paws tap the hardwood as we walked around and cleaned the house. I constantly dealt with thoughts of *what did I do wrong? What could I have done differently to save her? Did I do this to her? Did the poison from those years ago do this to her?*

Since her diagnosis, she was in and out of the pet hospital monthly. Towards the end of her life, it became weekly. I sobbed at night, trying to process what was happening. I would stay up late and watch her breathe, thankful she was right beside me and hopeless for what was to come. I watched and listened as it became harder for her to breathe. I prepared for the things I didn't even want to think about by researching urns, ways to grieve, looking up pet hospice tips, and making sure things were ready and in place. I had not felt the need to put her to sleep, even as I watched it become harder for her to breathe. She was still so playful, so vibrant, still talked with her sweet bark, and became excited when she saw her meal or I reached for the keys. She never lost her sense of personality, even on her most painful days.

That's the funny thing about love, I think. I don't know if it's a conscious effort or a subconscious effort, but I think we try and lessen the graveness of something we know we are going to lose. I look back on pictures and videos, and I see those tired eyes that lost just a little bit of that twinkle. I watched how hard she worked to love us and keep us happy. I try to think back on the times when I noticed that loss of twinkle in real life, and I don't recognize it. I loved her too much to even comprehend losing her. How can someone truly process that they are losing their entire world? She felt like my reason to breathe, the reason I woke up in the morning, and I wasn't going to lose my breath. We were just fine, I thought, even though there was a tiny, very tiny, little nagging feeling that the inevitable was coming sooner rather than later.

The winter of 2019 blew by. The snow came and went. While Pipi did go out and play in the snow sometimes, she was not always fond of the cold and winter wasn't her favorite season. She was a summer girl. Hikes and ponds and campfires and cuddles under the stars with a few snacks here and there, of course. Those were her favorite things.

Spring started to settle in. Life was looking very different for me than it had looked the previous spring. Pipi was a little grayer, and I had taken on a director position in my job. Still, Pipi trotted along right beside me day after day. My office was on the ground level. I had a window that led right out into an open area of grass. On the nice days of spring, when the sun was shining and she could warm her "piggy belly," as we affectionally called it, in the soft grass, I would throw open the window and set Pipi outside. She would sit outside the window and wallow around in the fresh green with such joy and gratefulness. The snow had melted, and her heart basked in the heat of the sun. Residents and staff loved watching Pipi lay outside my window. She was a funny sight to watch as she rolled and rolled with such exuberance on the renewed lawn.

I continued to have that nagging feeling that sooner was coming. But I always pushed it aside because Pipi never acted anything less than she was. It was so hard to see the truth with her grateful little body curled up in my arms. April soon arrived, bringing in rain, sunshine, and flowers. Pipi had developed a fond and curious fascination with window wells and flowers. We would walk around the building of our work and look at all the window wells and all the fresh new flowers on our breaks. Everything was fine, better than fine really, until April 16th.

April 12th, a typical Friday, would start the last weekend with my girl. These days, this feels like the most important part of our story together. If only I knew then what I know now. I had taken a four-day weekend just because I had felt like it. There was no reason to take the four days off, and I hadn't a clue why I was doing it. I guess that's how we all feel, though, when we lose someone so important to us. We replay our last moments together, good or bad. I came home from work that morning after working an overnight shift. We spent that Friday lounging around all day together. We ate our way through movies and tinkered around the house. We went on a walk around the block that evening and fell into bed snoozing away, satisfied with our lazy Friday together.

On Saturday my husband and I decided to take another hike with Pipi. We knew that we needed to keep the hike easy due to illness. We had purchased a stroller and a backpack to pack her in, both things she happily sat quietly in. We brought the backpack and went on a familiar trail near our house. Much to our surprise, Pipi was as spunky and bright as ever. It was like she was two years old again. She was prancing along the trail, hopping up and down rocks on her own, sniffing and smelling anything she could find. I stuck her in my backpack and scaled some small rocks with her like we had used to do. She sat quietly, looking around at all the openness. When we reached the top of a cliff, we sat and watched the world around us. It was quiet, peaceful, serene. We were happy. We were together.

With a lighter bounce in my foot, I felt on top of the world. My baby was fine. She was completely and totally fine. She was living her best life again. I had nothing to worry about for a long time. She is only nine years old. She has many years to live. Lots of people and animals live with heart conditions. My baby would conquer it all. Love would conquer it all.

We had a lazy Sunday. My husband and I spent the morning deep cleaning our home. You know that feeling when you have fresh sheets on the bed, the windows open with spring air filling the house, and all the clean dishes put away? That feeling you can just bask in the glow. It was made all the best by a little black pup snoozing quietly at the end of my freshly made, crisp white bed. My husband and I stood in the doorway, watching her dream. "This is perfect," I said out loud, and it truly was. We settled in for our *Game of Thrones* episode that night, popcorn in one hand and Pipi's movie snack in the other.

On Monday, April 15th, we spent the day with my mom. We lazed around in the morning. Went on random walks throughout the day. It was close to Easter, so we decided to donate some Easter baskets to the shelter. We went to the store to pick up some new toys, treats and food. My mom had brought Easter baskets and more toys to include in the gifts. We went to the shelter to drop off the toys and Pipi received so much attention and praise, just like she loved. She would pull her ears back, round her eyes into big puppy eyes, and hang her head humbly to gain the attention of anyone nearby. My mom loved on her the rest of the day. Napping with her on and off while I tinkered around the house. That night, my husband took her on her walk. I decided not to join them since I had taken her on walks earlier in the day. I wish I would have. I would give back anything to take her on her last walk again. But that's what we do in hindsight, we wish.

April 16th. I dressed for work, satisfied and grateful after a long, amazing weekend and a restful night of sleep. I wore black pants and a black and purple blouse, curled my hair, and slipped on my black flats. I still remember every detail of this day all these months later. Pipi snoozed quietly on the bed, although her breathing seemed harsher than usual. I gave her some extra Furosemide that morning to see if that would help. She continued to breathe harshly. I called my husband and told him to come to take her to the vet as I had to get to work. I believed this was just another trip to the vet, one we had been doing bi-weekly at this point. I kissed her goodbye, told her I loved her and walked out the door.

I drove the half hour to work when I received a call right when I arrived at my office. "It's not good. You need to come back." Instant panic set in. "Why, what's wrong? Is she dying?" I asked quickly, tears already forming. "It's not good," my husband whispered over the phone. My mom had come from work to pick Pipi up from the vet and bring her back home so my husband could go straight back to work. I could hear her sobbing quietly in the background.

I raced to my car and drove as fast as I could to the clinic. I was over an hour away from her. An hour of her life I would not get to spend with her. I felt disoriented as I sobbed. "Not today, Lord. Please not today. I'm not ready," I cried out loud. I prayed as hard as I could all the way to the clinic. An hour of panic, heart-shattering, head-spinning confusion. How could this be happening? We had the best weekend. She was perfect. "How is this happening? This isn't real." I sobbed over and over as I sped to the clinic. My husband called several more times, telling me to hurry. When I arrived at the clinic, I entered the room, and I didn't think my heart could hurt any more than it did. Pipi was lying in my husband's arms. His face was glistening from the tears. I had never seen him cry before, and he cried now as he rocked his dying baby in his arms. My mom was in the corner of the room, face bright red and tears streaming down her face.

"Her body temperature is significantly lower than it should be. Her organs are probably shutting down. We've wrapped her in warm blankets and continued to check her temperature. It's time to look at euthanizing her." I let out a big heavy sob. Euthanize.

"I'm not ready yet!" I cried, tears streaming freely down my face.

"No one is ever ready," my mom choked out through her own tears.

I held Pipi's face in my hands. I could barely process what was happening.

"Can I take her on a walk in her stroller one last time? And can we do it outside? She's her calmest outside," I asked quietly. The vets agreed.

The sun was shining brightly. The weather was a gorgeous high 60s out. The day was still. We walked her for a few minutes in her stroller, letting her soak up the sun one last time and sniffing the air like she enjoyed. Her button nose wiggled around like a rabbit's as she breathed in the morning air.

I set her down to go potty, the Furosemide running its course. She coughed as she went. My heart sunk. This was really it. She's tired. At nine years old, her body was failing her. She held on as long as she could.

The vets were waiting for us in a gazebo outside. I wrapped her up in her favorite blanket, sat in a chair, and set her on my lap one last time. My mom cradled her head in her hands, and my husband stood beside us and gently petted her. I whispered to her how much I loved her all throughout the process. I told her all the plans I had for us that summer. I kissed her goodbye.

I had never done anything harder in my life than saying goodbye to that girl.

Life after Pipi was difficult. That day my husband and I went home and stared at the wall for hours. There was nothing we could say or do to bring her back or offer each other comfort. When your entire schedule revolves around someone and that someone is just gone, adjusting is hard. No more pills to make sure she got at certain times of the day, no more extra dinner to make for her, no more tucking her into bed, no more making sure she got playtime or nap time. No more buying her the best toys in the store. No more appointments to make for her. It all disappeared in just a few minutes. Everything just stopped but the world didn't stop, and I couldn't figure out how to spin with it.

I spent many days in bed after she was gone. I didn't return to work for a while. My mom was worried about me. I had stopped eating, stopped being. It sounds so silly to love a dog that much. But there was such a deep, soul-binding connection. I couldn't grasp how to go on without it.

My mom suggested we get another dog. My mom is a dog groomer and she felt it helped to be around other dogs after Pipi's passing.

"Another dog will bring you light again. A reason to go on walks," she tried to convince me.

I knew I wanted to adopt from a shelter. As the week went by, I happened to come across a listing for a chorkie puppy on Facebook. I debated on if I wanted another chorkie puppy. Would I compare this puppy? Do I even want a puppy? I wanted to adopt from the shelter. I did not want to buy a puppy. I requested a hold on the puppy. I didn't believe she was real.

"The puppy is already alive and needs a home," my mom commented. "If it's meant to be, she will be there when you get there."

The puppy was in Nashville, nine hours from our home. I loved to travel and my husband thought it might be a great excuse to get out of the house that was haunting me. We packed our bags and took off. I was reluctant that entire trip, not believing we would be bringing a puppy home. This was just a good trip to get my mind off the sudden loss.

We spent the weekend in Nashville and on the last day of our trip, contacted the woman with the puppy to see if the puppy was still there. She was. We drove to the woman's home, which was not in good condition. The woman handed the very frightened puppy to me quickly. She was covered in urine and smelled terrible. She trembled in my arms. There were no parents around. No siblings. Nothing but the puppy and her tiny cage. As soon as we got into the car, the puppy vomited all over the blanket. Now our nine-hour car ride back home would smell like vomit and pee. It was going to be a long one.

We stopped at a PetSmart, and I washed her off in the sink as my husband washed off her blanket. That's when I noticed she couldn't walk. My heart sunk, thoughts racing of the condition she came from and what life must have been like for her. I washed her off, bought her some snacks and toys, and we continued our way. I set her on my lap, put the stuffed animal beside her, and covered them both in a blanket. She slept the entire carried home.

We stopped frequently to have her stretch her legs and try and get her to go potty. The first time we set her in the grass, she was extremely frightened and tried to move. She couldn't move, whether from being so frightened or from something that happened to her in her short little 10 weeks of age. We had to carry her around. She never once did use the potty break. She just sat quietly in the grass each time. When we arrived home, my mom swooped her up in her arms. "I like her," she said instantly.

My mom worked with her the days after that. She stretched her, massaged her, and gave her incentives to try and move around. Eventually, she did start to move. These days we have a very healthy, very spunky, very ornery little girl named Scout. She loves any and all other dogs that she encounters, big or small. She is still scared of most humans, and we're working on that. She is still a full puppy and likes to chew on everything and falls asleep in the oddest places at the most random times. She just graduated puppy kindergarten, and everyone was so proud of her.

It's been a difficult road. There are days when I cry to have Pipi back, and I must shoo away thoughts of comparison between the two of them. There are so many similarities between Pipi and Scout. They like and dislike the same snacks, play in the same manner, share the same face, and curl up in the same spots around the house. But there are many differences too. We're learning to love and appreciate their sibling status, loving two very similar yet very different dogs. It's so fun to see the world through a puppy's eyes again. Everything is so new, so joyful, so pain-free, like dandelions or bumblebees. Apparently, those are very tasty too! Who knew?

I still like to talk to her about her sister and in some ways, I think she understands. Grief is such a hard, messy thing to deal with. It's been a turning point in my short 25 years of life though. Pipi taught me so much during her life and after her life too. I've come to realize that as hopeful as I was for grief to pass, it won't. Grief is a mark we all must learn to live with daily, but we learn to work around the scar too. It won't ever go away, and we'll always remember why it's there, but we learn to live with it somehow. I miss Pipi more than words will ever be able to say but Scout is wiggling her way into our hearts each and every day.

Pipi

The Story of Daisy
The Love of My Life
By Marie Bowman

My love for dachshunds goes back to my childhood. My parents weren't dog people, so I never had one growing up. When I got married, I soon discovered my husband was not a dog person either, so we always had cats, but I always wanted a dachshund. When my daughter turned 18 years old in 2008, she was going to move into an apartment with a friend and brought home this little, brown long-hair dachshund puppy named Lou. I was 44 years old and fell in love with him, as did my husband, and needless to say, she moved into her apartment, and we became dog parents. After having him for a year, we decided to adopt him as a friend. This is the beginning of my journey with the love of my life, Daisy.

We didn't know about puppy mills at that time, so we started looking online at the same place my daughter purchased Lou. We saw one we loved and put a deposit on her. She was a smooth black and tan dachshund. I always wanted a smooth-haired. A week later, we drove an hour to the breeders to pick her up and they walked out with a tiny little chocolate girl. I told them this was not the puppy I put a deposit on and they told me the other one was gone. I was about to go off at them (as I was known to do back them). Then he handed her to me. We looked into each other's eyes and it was love at first sight. She had a cold and smelled awful, but I didn't care, she had to be mine. It turned out she was Lou's half-sister as they had the same father. She spent the ride home wrapped around the back of my neck and our journey began.

It didn't take long to figure out who her favorite human was. She was my shadow, she was everywhere I was. She was a feisty little thing, full of piss and vinegar. During her first few months with us, she spent every night sleeping across my throat until she was too big; then she switched to curling up on my pillow around my head. As the years went on, I realized that we could tell what the other was thinking.

The best thing about Daisy was that every day was new and exciting. It didn't matter what we were doing as long as we were together. I love music and so did she. As soon as I would turn on the music, I had to pick her up and we would dance together. She had favorite songs too. There was always dancing and singing when she was with me. I would sing You Are My Sunshine to her every night before we went to sleep and her little eyes would start to close, she would make a deep sigh and fall sound asleep because all was right in the world at that very moment.

She also loved everything about being outside; the sun, rolling in the grass, but she especially loved the birds and squirrels. I swear that girl could sit in one spot for an hour and not move just waiting for the squirrel to come over the fence. She knew exactly where they came from and would just stare at that spot. Sometimes she would get lucky and a squirrel would forget we were out there and jump the fence to try to get to the feeder. She would take off like a rocket. I always joked that one day, fire was going to come out of her butt upon takeoff. I didn't know those short little legs could move so fast. Of course, the squirrel would run along the fence with her chasing behind barking all along the way. When it was over, she would come running to me as if she were saying, *Did you see that, Mom?* I would just look at her and say, *I know.*

During the spring and summer, she wanted to be outside all the time. I needed to do something to justify all of the time in the backyard, so I decided to take up gardening. I had a blank canvas to work with as the backyard was just fence and grass. We did have an 18-foot round patch of sand where the pool used to be, so I started with that. I built a patio over the sand, then came the plants and shrubs around it. It turned out beautiful and we now had a spot to sit and watch the world go by. We would work in the garden by day and sit on the patio swing, with her wrapped in a blanket, in the evening and wait for the bats to come out. They would fly over our heads just at dusk and she would look at me when they did with her big brown eyes and I would say, *I know*.

Each year, we worked on a different side of the yard. She had to inspect every hole I dug. She helped me weed; I would dig around it and tell her to pull it out and she would. It was so funny watching her pull that thing with all her might. Sometimes she would get tired and would find a warm spot to take a little nap and then wake up and be ready to continue.

My favorite memory in the garden was the evening I divided a yucca and transplanted the pieces into one of the beds. She helped as usual and when they were all planted, I moved on to something else. A few minutes later, I turned around to see what she was doing only to find that she had dug each piece up and placed them in a neat pile as if she were saying, *Let's do it again, Mom*. She was so proud of herself, all I could do was laugh. She loved when I laughed. We spent seven years together laughing and creating that garden.

Another thing she loved to do was go on walks. As soon as she saw the leash and harness, she would scream with excitement and of course piddle. It took longer to get the harness on her than the actual walk I think. We took the same route every time and each day was like she had never been that way before. She would start out running and making the cutest excitement cry, but then she would get a little tired and slow to a walk. We had to stop and inspect each and every sewer grate along the way. She would sniff and sniff and I would always tell her to be so careful because doggies could fall in. I would always let her walk as long as she wanted. She never wanted to turn around; she always wanted to go forward. She would walk and walk and walk. When she had enough, she would just drop to the ground on the grass. She was done. Of course, I would have to carry her back home. For a little dog, she was quite solid and heavy. She was 18-pounds and here I was carrying her back home. It was the same thing all the time but I didn't mind one bit. We were together enjoying the great outdoors.

The winters were different. She would sleep by the fireplace in the daytime and hang out on the couch with me cuddled in a blanket in the evenings watching TV. She would let me know when it was time for bed and off we would go. There were mornings I didn't even want to get out of bed because it felt so peaceful just lying there with her by my side. She didn't like when I went to work, but my husband is disabled and was always home with her and the pack, (I have three other dogs) so she got used to me leaving five days a week. When I would get home, she was the first one at the door to greet me. She would do this unusual thing where she would grab my left thumb in her mouth and wouldn't let go. She had done this from a puppy, it was like she was telling me to not leave her again. She would get so excited she would let out a scream and a little piddle. Every day was the same.

We almost became one. The only way I can describe our relationship is to refer to the movie *E.T.* when Elliot started feeling everything E.T. was feeling and they were able to communicate. It was magical. She never did grow out of her "stink," but I grew to love that smell. I don't think I will ever have the same relationship with anyone – human or canine – as I did with her. I was happy when I was with her. She was so full of love; I could feel the love coming from her.

December 2017 was the beginning of the end of our journey together. I had felt that something was wrong with her for a few weeks. I couldn't put my finger on it but she just wasn't right. I brought her to the vet the week before Christmas for a complete physical as I told him my thoughts. He gave her a thorough exam and determined she was fine. I brought her home knowing something was off. Looking back on that day, I wonder why he didn't do blood work and why I didn't think to suggest it.

That whole next week she declined fast. Overnight she developed a huge bulge on the right side of her neck. I didn't get to see my regular vet as we were squeezed in and the doctor that was there took one look at her and said, "Oh no." He said it over and over as he checked this giant lump. He couldn't believe it grew so big overnight. I remember thinking at the time, this guy was a real piece of work. Why did he have to be so dramatic? I would soon find out. He said to get her to Ohio State Veterinary Hospital immediately as they are a teaching hospital and have the best equipment and staff. He phoned ahead to let them know we were coming. It was bad, they thought she had cancer. They did surgery to biopsy it and discovered it was her salivary gland. They removed it and put her on phenobarbital. Her blood numbers kept dropping and she would come home only to crash and go back to the hospital. She was in and out of the hospital five times. Seven thousand dollars and two months later, they determined she had an autoimmune disease that was attacking her blood and she couldn't be saved. It was time to let her go.

February 24th, 2018. I will remember that day for the rest of my life. It is embedded in my brain. She was only eight and the love of my life. How could this be happening? Why was God doing this to us? We were supposed to spend our golden years together. We had plans and yet, in one sentence, everything was going to end. They led us into an exam room and brought her in to us, she was all wrapped up in a blanket. My husband said his goodbyes and left the room as he was afraid his heart couldn't take it. I can't get the picture out of my head of her eyes watching him leave the room. It haunts me to this day and probably will for the rest of my life. The rest of it is kind of a blur as it happened so fast. I was hysterical, there was no consoling me. I felt like my heart was going to burst out of my chest; I was shaking and had a horrible headache. I held her tight, told her I loved her and to go find her grandpa in Heaven. She looked at me with those beautiful brown eyes and one last time I said, *I know*. I told the doctor I was ready to let her go. She administered the injection and was gone. She asked me if I wanted some time with her and I remember saying that she was gone, and I needed to go outside and scream. When I handed her over, her head fell off my shoulder and I just fell to the floor. This was real, she was gone. They let me out the back door and I met my husband outside. He grabbed me and put his arms around me and I just lost it. I remember saying over and over, what am I going to do without her? I can't do this without her. When we turned onto our street, we were driving into the most beautiful sunset I have ever seen. My husband said that was Daisy letting us know that God opened the gates and she made it safely to the Rainbow Bridge. She was telling me she was okay, and it was beautiful there.

Now what? I am home and she isn't here. She was the light of my life and now my world had gone dark. I already missed her warmth and the way she smelled. I took the next day off of work to let myself grieve. I was a mess. I couldn't go outside in the backyard without crying so I stayed away from there for a while. I've always heard people say that they felt empty inside and I never really understood that feeling until my girl was gone. I felt empty and numb, I still do. Everything was suddenly different. Music sounded different, the air smelled different, food tasted different. Even watching television felt different because she wasn't sitting on the couch with me. We used to watch *Ghost Adventures* together and she would get all excited when I would tell her it was time to watch our "ghosty" show. She knew exactly what that meant. Her tail would wag uncontrollably, and she would let out a little piddle. I haven't watched that show since she died.

I'm different now. I'm not sure if my friends, family, and co-workers notice it because I do a pretty good job of hiding my grief, but I am a different person, always carrying around that emptiness. I don't enjoy the things I used to and I haven't really found anything that makes me truly happy. Right after she left, I threw myself into a giant home remodel which I have been doing all alone to keep myself occupied during my free time. I've painted just about every room in the house, pulled up carpets and put down new flooring, painted kitchen cabinets, painted furniture, and there is still so much more to do. It has become an obsession. I never allowed myself to finish grieving; just that one day and then I turned it off. Keeping busy is what keeps me sane.

I started a memory garden for her last year but couldn't finish it right away. I did manage to complete it this spring in between home projects, but that too was difficult to get done. Someone told me to not be sad about it, but to cherish it because her memory will live on in the garden and everything I planted in the yard with her. It's mostly finished now but I haven't just sat in the yard at all this summer. I have no desire to be out there except to work. I keep it pristine as a way to honor her memory. I'm still hoping there will come a day when it brings me joy instead of sorrow. She is in the back of my mind every waking minute. I am so afraid that there will be a day I wake up and not think of her. I feel like I would be betraying her in some way and that scares the hell out of me.

I know a meltdown is coming. You can't hold all that grief inside and go about your day forever. I don't know exactly how to explain it but I constantly feel like I am holding it all back and it is right there at the surface. It is exhausting, holding this heavy load back and I know that one day I am going to let my guard down, just for a minute, and it is going to erupt like a volcano, and I don't know what will happen.

Every day I have a strange feeling that something is missing. It's kind of like when you realize you don't have your purse on your shoulder or left home without your wallet.

She hasn't come to me in a dream yet, but she has given me signs. About a week after she passed away, a light bulb popped and burned out. As I walked over to it, I realized Pandora was playing, "Sunshine on my Shoulders," by John Denver. I would always sing, "You Are My Sunshine," to her and wondered if that could be a sign from Daisy. The very next day another light bulb did the same thing and at that moment

Pandora was playing, "Bridge Over Troubled Water," by Simon & Garfunkel, and I realized that it had to be her. The lyrics to both of those songs are so beautiful and completely convey the relationship we had. I feel as though she is still communicating with me and is telling me she is at peace and still with me. The last song, "Reminds Me of You," by Van Morrison; I think the universe sent me that song because it's so sad and describes how much I miss Daisy – I hope she hears it when it's playing.

I know she has sent me birds, butterflies, dragonflies, hummingbirds, and feathers. They seem to appear just when I need a sign from her the most. Those things make me happy and I always say, *Thank you, Daisy,* and feel at peace in those moments. But those moments are very short-lived. I just miss her.

I had a vet appointment for one of my other dogs tonight and got to see the vet who saw Daisy the day it all began. He was the one who told me to take her to the hospital right away. It's the first time I have spoken with him since then. He remembered her immediately and told me things I didn't know were going on with her immune system during those two months she was in and out of the hospital. It was a series of events that just kept occurring. It started with her salivary gland and the medication to keep it under control attacked her blood and then she started having seizures that were affecting her nervous system. It was one thing after another. I asked him if anything could have saved her, but he told me no. She was a very rare case and they had never seen anything like it before. They are still talking about her as OSU is a teaching hospital and there are multiple case studies. She is going to be in veterinary medical journals; there will be papers written about her condition and much research done in the next few years. He also told me if he ever comes across any research as a result of her case, he will give me a copy. He said that she didn't die in vain and her life and death will eventually help save other animals. Hearing that gave me the push I needed to finish this story. I knew she was a special dog and maybe, just maybe, this is why she was so special – this will be her legacy. I always knew she was sent here for a reason. She completely changed me. I was mean and angry before she came into my life but was able to let that go because of watching the world through her eyes for eight years, and I will forever be grateful to her for that. I just haven't been able to figure out why she was taken from me so soon. She was able to change me when no one else could and if her illness and passing can save just one dog, then I guess it was meant to be. They always say God has a plan.

I had her cremated and set up a little memorial on my dresser. She is the first thing I see when I wake up in the morning and the last thing I see when I go to sleep at night. I'm not afraid of death anymore because I know she will be waiting for me. When I die, I will also be cremated and her ashes will be mixed with mine so we can finally be together for all eternity. Until that day, I will just continue to miss her and remember all of the fun we had during our time together here on this earth.

I love you Miss Daisy and will miss you and remember you until I take my last breath. Rest peacefully my beautiful girl, I am forever changed because of you. Until we meet again.

Daisy

A Love Letter to My Music
By Maude Moreno

Dear Music (my baby girl, my little girl, my daughter), I remember the first time I saw you. We were at the Nebraska Humane Society, not really looking for anyone in particular. We had no idea what breed, color, or sex to look for, just that we wanted a small to medium-sized dog who would be a lap dog. I had been telling your daddy, "I want a dog that can calm me down and encourage me to stay home and sit instead of running around."

We enter one of the rooms and I distinctly remember you being on my right side. You were lying on one of those humongous dog beds with your back to me. But instead of looking ahead, you kept looking behind you, watching each person walk by. I was one of those people "perusing" one kennel after another. I saw you and I right away thought, she's so cute and beautiful. I remember stopping outside your kennel a little bit longer. I cooed you to approach me but you wouldn't. You just had a blank look on your face.

I walked on but I didn't get to the end of the hall. I remember backpedaling back to you. This time, I sat outside your kennel like the trainer encouraged us to and kept calling your name so you would approach me. You were named Cali, or was it, Callie? I don't really remember.

All of a sudden, the other dogs were howling and barking and the whole place got riotous. Yet there you were. Sitting quietly. And you were supposed to be a Chihuahua?

I asked to have some private time with you in the meeting room. I sat down with my legs crossed. You came in, and surveyed all the corners of the room with your head and tail down. Then just like that, you came to me and sat on my legs. And that was it. It was love, we were inseparable. Did you know that I asked your daddy, "On a scale of 1 to 10, how much are you feeling her?" He said, "Zero."

Boy, did he quickly learn how wrong he was. We had never had a dog as a couple before, so we learned everything from you. We learned:

That we could step on your feet easily if we didn't look where we were going.

That you were destined to sleep on our bed since day one no matter how we resisted.

That you chewed on plastic cords and cables.

That you inhaled anything edible in front of you.

That you knew you were the most beautiful baby.

That you would be at the vet your first two weeks with us because we were so careless about a box of chocolates just laying around.

That you would be waiting by the basement door for eight. Freaking. Hours. Every. Day.

That your "dog smell" would turn into our most favorite scent in the world.

That your bottom teeth looked as crooked as mine.

That you were just content being in my presence.

That plenty of times we would cancel all plans just so we could stay at home with you.

That we would get another dog because we didn't want you all alone at home.

That you would have no qualms being in a backpack.

That you could jump from one couch to another when excited.

That you had a luxating patella that didn't seem to be a huge issue to you.

That we had to really watch your weight. Like, really really watch your weight.

That cradling you in my arms was going to be a nightly ritual.

That you would be on my Yoga mat every time I would practice at home.

That we loved taking you and Cadence with us on road trips and missed you like crazy when we were out of the country.

That somehow you had the ability to warm up to other dogs and people when we were not around.

That we felt safe in the middle of the night knowing you would bark at the faintest sound.

That we would look forward to napping with you.

That you hated 90% of all our male guests.

That you hated it when we slept late and would wait for us by the bedroom door.

That you had the most powerful, sonorous tail wag.

That you had the highest tolerance for pain according to all the vets we saw.

That you would let us do anything to you. *Anything*. Including puppeteering.

That we would get very good at anthropomorphizing.

That you would give your daddy unrequited love.

That you would love me like no one ever has. And ever will.

That I would unabashedly call you, my daughter.

But there are a few things we did not learn until much later. We didn't learn that your heart was a little bigger than it should be.

That you would have heightened liver enzymes.

That you had a dormant anemia condition called IMHA which your daddy and I can now define because the doctor would always say the longer version of it.

That by the time we had to take you to the hospital that Tuesday, April 16th, you had already had four to five strokes within the past month.

That when you lost your appetite those first few days it was probably when you had your first stroke.

That when your appetite returned, that was part of you either healing or just having that super high tolerance for pain.

That when you would stop walking it wasn't because of your patella. Something else was going on.

I am so sorry we could not fix your condition. I am so sorry we could not address it earlier. I am so sorry about our ignorance about your condition. I am so sorry we could not visit you as often as we wanted to in the ICU.

But the whole time you were there, we were also very grateful for a lot of things. We were so grateful every time you wagged your tail because that must have taken every effort. That as much as it was hard for us to see you in that state, it must have been harder for you to see us and not come home with us every single night of those nine whole nights you were there. I often wonder and ask these questions:

Did you know what was going on?

How much of us did you see with your vision being compromised?

At what time of the night did your final stroke happen?

How long had it been going on when your daddy saw you shaking?

Did you feel my fear when I was crying in the back of the car while daddy rushed you to the ER?

Did you feel abandoned every time we left the ICU?

Were you trying to tell us to stop every time we dragged your butt to walk?

Did it hurt?

Did you mean to pass away on my mom's birthday?

When we asked you to give us a sign that you were ready to go, you decided to close your eyes and sleep. You even snored. In the whole ten days you were in the ICU, that was the first time you had looked so peaceful. As if you were ready and were making it easy for us.

A day after you passed, I saw a hummingbird outside our bathroom window. Two days later, your daddy did. We had never seen a hummingbird outside our window at 8:30 a.m. Ever. We got eight double egg yolks up until the 11th day after you passed. At some point, we got three in one day. The bedroom, kitchen, and bathroom lights would flicker more than they normally did. A ladybug flew right off our red tree in the backyard and onto my arm.

I saw your tail "float" towards our bedroom one night. I felt your weight press against that space between my legs which became your favorite place in the whole world to sleep.

We connected with an animal communicator who told us that you are going to be attached to me for quite a while and things will be that way as long as I am not ok. That you are still very much around, closer than I think even. And as long as I am not ok, you will not be able to move on to the next "thing." More importantly, she said that you wanted to come back to me, probably in dog form (which is good because I am allergic to cats). Is that true, baby girl? Are we really going to be together again? Despite our shortcomings and foresight, do you really want to reunite and rekindle our devoted love for each other in the future? What are you going to look like? How are we going to know? What signs will you give us? Why haven't you shown up in my dreams?

My baby girl, I got a tattoo of both your paws on my shoulders and your nose behind my one ear. I had a ring made out of a picture of you. I got an urn necklace with a pendant shaped like a musical note and I put your ashes inside. I had a blanket made out of a collage of your photos. Then I had a pillow made that I kiss and hug to sleep every night. I also came up with an email address for you just so I could write to you anytime I wanted to. Which is what I am doing right now, only it will be part of a book. Funny how something so personal to me is going to be read by people who never had the pleasure of meeting you. These pages are a big slice of my soul because that was what you were and still are. A big slice of my soul.

I will never be the same person because of you, little girl. Nor will your daddy. You have taught us lesson after lesson, made us laugh after laugh, and allowed us to love in ways we did not know how.

So let me end this by saying the very same words we uttered on your last day: we are sorry. Please forgive us. We thank you. We love you.

Until we see each other again. We miss you in ways words will not be able to describe.
Mommy

Music

My Little Confidant
By Rhi White

The morning of December 29th, 2018, will be forever etched in my brain.

My baby girl was named Izzy, and she was the cutest and most loving little creature I have ever had the pleasure of meeting. She had a hard start in life, being stolen from her then family for the purpose of breeding. She was a Plummer terrier which, at the time, was an incredibly rare breed. She was too young, still a puppy herself when she had her own litter and it almost killed her. She was no use to the breeders anymore, so she was dumped outside and urgently needed a hysterectomy; it was very touch and go for a while but her owners were found and reunited.

Izzy was very flighty and excitable. She got out of their house one day and ran away, that's when my family found her outside in deep snow. We took her home and looked for her owners who happened to live just down the road from us and took her back. We knew it was the right thing to do but it was very hard giving her back because even though we had known her just a couple of days we had bonded.

A few days later there was a knock at the door and there was Izzy with her owner, the lady explained that Izzy hadn't settled back in with them and asked if we would like to keep her.

It was only then we found out about her tough beginning. From that day on we were inseparable. I truly believe that Izzy was meant for us.

Izzy was very happy to be 'home' with us. She may have had a rough start in life but from then on, she was treated like a queen. She thought she ruled the house and if I'm being completely honest, she did. My friends talked about their children, I talked about Izzy. She used to go and have a sleepover at her "grandparents" house on Saturdays, including coming along with us for visits to other family members. On my days off of work, I used to go to my Nan's and cook dinner for her. Izzy would come along and there was always a sausage in it for her.

Izzy's flighty side surfaced from time to time. We had her too late in life to properly train her so although she was great on lead, she saw being off lead as a means to stretch her legs and run as fast as she could. Thankfully, she did have road sense though. She used to sneak past us as we left the house sometimes, it was the fastest I ever ran but she never ran too far so I couldn't catch and carry her home with her tail between the legs.

At one time, while my husband's friend was living in our spare room, he let her out but didn't go after her. He told me she ran away when I got home from work and my husband and I spent the evening frantically searching for her. I also spent the night on my settee with the front door open in case she made her way back home. We searched for two more days before we had a call to say she was at a local shelter. As we drove up the hill to pick her up, we see Izzy running down with shelter staff running after her. My little Houdini is still the only dog I've ever heard of escaping the pound. My little tough Nut never ran away again, I think she learned a lesson and didn't want to lose us.

She may have been a tiny dog but she had bundles of personality. She certainly made her presence known.

Izzy was with me through a lot of hard times in my life. I lost my Nan, my mother-in-law, three aunties, and an uncle in just under a year. During this time, I began my battle with anxiety and depression, I still battle to this day. Izzy was always there when I needed her. I received so much emotional support from her.

After the shock of my mother-in-law passing away, suddenly at a young age I was diagnosed with fibromyalgia. I also have multiple other health conditions which have left me very disabled and unable to work. I had to finish from a job I had invested ten years of my life at and again Izzy supported me. She was right by my side. Some days when I am in too much pain to get out of bed, she would be my only company as my husband works long hours.

Over the past year, Izzy had started to slow down and her ginger face had gradually turned white, she was becoming very frail. Although in hindsight there were warning signs of her aging, it was still a tremendous shock when we lost her. That was the morning of the 29th of December.

The night before, my husband and I had been at a party for my mother's 60th birthday. When we arrived home, Izzy was completely normal. She just gave us a 'kiss' and fell asleep in her usual spot on my feet. She always kept them warm for me. My husband woke up for work at 5:00 a.m. and Izzy was completely fine even then. I woke up at approximately 8:30 a.m. and Izzy was whimpering. I looked and she had swollen up.

I rang the vet and my mother took me down with Izzy, I rang my husband to meet us there. The vet took one look at her and told us her organs were shutting down due to old age. We had to have her put to sleep. By 11:00 a.m. my baby was gone.

The image of her life leaving her body as they injected her haunts me. I just cannot shift it. My poor husband was holding her and has since told me that he felt her heart stop beating. We brought her home with us to bury her in the garden. I held her for what seemed like hours and I just felt numb.

After she was buried, I just sat staring into space. My husband's way of dealing with the situation was to try and remove items that could trigger memories from sight. He threw out her bed and her bowls. I know he was only trying to help me, but I do wish we would have kept some of her things.

All I have left is her collar and her favourite toy who we called Hoopy. Izzy would always stand with us at the top of our stairs, waiting for us to throw Hoopy so she could run down and fetch it.

One day, Izzy worked out that she could nudge or paw Hoopy down the stairs herself. She would throw it down and fetch it for herself over and over. It was great having a dog who could keep herself entertained until she decided to play at 2:00 a.m. and wake both me and my husband with Hoopy clattering down the stairs. I would give anything to be awoken by that again.

Life hasn't been the same since. I feel like I live my life in a blur. I have cried so much that I wonder how my tear ducts haven't run dry. Sometimes I find myself catching my breath and it feels like it physically hurts. Then comes the guilt. The guilt of crying more for Izzy than I have for some people I've lost.

Then you start to search for reasons. I found evidence of a chocolate bar that Izzy must have gotten hold of at some point. A chocolate bar I had put on a shelf that I thought was too high for her to get to. She couldn't even get on the bed without help and the shelf was much higher than that. I have no clue how she managed to get to it.

I started to blame myself for Izzy's death, I still do to some extent. My little girl deserved so much more after the support she gave me and I failed her in the worst possible way.

Since that day, family and friends have tried to convince me that it was not my fault. After all, I did not feed her the chocolate. Also, the evidence of chocolate being the cause of her death is very circumstantial many of them say. It's just too circumstantial for me. It doesn't matter what I try to tell myself or how I try to look at it, I keep coming back to it being my fault.

The *what-ifs* keep haunting me. What if I had been more careful with the chocolate? What if I had noticed the chocolate before I took her to the vet? I keep wondering if they could have saved her if they had all the information to make a medical diagnosis. I'm afraid it will haunt me for the rest of my life.

I have given it a lot of thought. As time goes by, my thoughts become more rational. I think back to Izzy's previous antics, one story in particular from a few years back. I remember it being early December when I came home from work to find two empty advent calendars and one very sheepish Izzy. As she was younger at the time, the chocolate didn't affect her at all, I have come to the conclusion that her age was definitely a factor in her death but I still feel that I shortened her life in some way.

Sleeping has been very difficult. I have a microwaveable teddy which I sleep with. If I closed my eyes and felt the warmth from it, I could fool myself that it was Izzy. I understand that may not have been healthy but at the very beginning, it was the only way I could get any sleep. It still didn't stop the nightmares though; I wake crying in the night frequently.

I do wonder how much one family is meant to endure because every time I begin to pick myself up something else knocks me back down again. This time seems even harder in some ways because my little girl isn't by my side anymore to help me. Looking into her eyes, that somehow knew just what to say, would never fail to make me feel that much better because I could tackle anything with Izzy's unconditional love to help me.

The loss of a pet somehow seems different from the loss of a person. When I have lost people I have had other people to be strong for, but there was nobody closer to Izzy than me and I have just crumbled. As time goes by, the grief just randomly hits you for no apparent reason and brings you to your knees sobbing. I loved Izzy like she was my child, with my health like it is I don't think I will ever be well enough to have children so she kind of filled that void. She has left a huge, gaping hole in my life.

Around two weeks after Izzy's passing, I went for a day out with my family and it was the first time I had felt anywhere close to my normal self. I came home and called for Izzy. It was only then I thought about it and realised she wasn't there anymore. It was almost like losing her all over again. I felt sick.

I miss hearing her trot around the house, I miss our cuddles, I miss her making me look like a furball, I miss our friendship, I miss being a mammy, I miss her strength, and I miss the person she made me. There is a quote I come back to quite regularly:

I miss you.
A little too much,
a little too often
and a little more
every day.

This seems to sum up my feelings perfectly. I try to remain positive that I had her in my life long enough to see her bright ginger face turn white because some are not that lucky. Now looking back, it just reduces me to tears. I am crying as I write this, but I hope in time I will be able to look back at our memories and smile or even laugh.

I have been having a battle with myself about getting another dog. I feel that I need the company, but I feel like I'd be 'replacing' Izzy. I know if I do, I will get a shelter dog. A dog cannot leave a will, but I truly believe if they could, they would ask for another fur baby to have a happy life. I am thinking of honouring Izzy's life by giving another pet a home. Some nights I just really need my baby. She will never be here again, but that doesn't stop me from needing her. I wonder if another dog will help.

My husband and I sent a form to request to meet a brother and sister called Dexter and Beau. They were beautiful dogs. We arranged a meeting, but my husband was wondering if I was requesting to meet them purely out of desperation rather than the correct reasons, and in hindsight he was right.

My husband voiced his concerns and convinced me to cancel the meeting. I was very upset and at the time couldn't understand his reasoning. We had both spoken to shelter staff separately, but once we spoke about it together, we found that we had been given conflicting information about the dogs. I was annoyed because I had explained that I was disabled and would need the dogs to be fairly self-sufficient in regard to playing. My husband was told that they were known to fight, and the new owner would need to be able to split them up which I would not be.

By not informing me of this, it caused more heartache as I was set on adopting Dexter and Beau. I cried over them, but really, I was crying over Izzy once again as that awfully familiar feeling of having a dog taken from you in some way came back to the forefront.

My husband and I have since been in touch with a different shelter about a gorgeous little girl named Sally. We have met her twice and have a home visit scheduled for her to see our house. I did worry at first if I was meeting her for the wrong reasons again because she is the spitting image of Izzy, but all those fears melted away when I met her. I warmed up to her in seconds, as did my husband. We have everything crossed that all goes well in the adoption process.

I do hope that Izzy doesn't feel betrayed, those fears are still there in the back of my head. I believe that above anything else though, Izzy would want us to be happy and I feel that Sally could bring some joy and comfort back into our lives.

It's now been six months without Izzy, and it feels like so much longer. My heart breaks a little more each day. There are lots of things I'm just not strong enough to do yet, one being decorating her grave. There are stones on top of where she is buried, which I plan to paint and make her resting place as beautiful as she was.

I will love you forever baby girl. Run and play until we meet again.

Izzy

Kanook (2005-2016) & Shasta (2009-2018)
By Sharon

I will never forget the day I brought you home. Such a beautiful boy, true husky colours with the most beautiful blue eyes; you were six weeks old with attitude to burn. Kanook, also known as Cookie or Cookie Monster, you became.

As the weeks flew by, you wormed your way into my bed and my heart. The first time you were skating around the kitchen, one paw on your dog biscuit, who couldn't help but laugh.

My son wanted to take you to town, when I asked why he said, "He is a chick magnet, Mum." Um no.

My relationship broke down and we moved to town, it was just you and me, you were four months old. I woke up one night to find you between me and the wooden sides of the bed with your paws against the wood so I couldn't push you out of bed, or the time there was an intruder in our back yard, and you were out there bouncing around him wanting to play; a watchdog you were not, but you would have given your life for me.

You were never a naughty dog – almost never. There was the time I came home from work to find you peering around the corner at me. What have you done, Kanook? You would pull your head back behind the door, then peek out at me again when

I walked into the garage. I saw what you had done: four litres of engine oil spread all through the garage. But who could be angry with those big blue eyes?

Over the next four years, we went through so much together, you always stood beside me no matter what. We ended up homeless and jobless at one stage and I had to leave you for a few weeks until I got a job and a house for us; I was heartbroken without you.

If you were displeased with me for any reason, I sure would know about it. The time I was going to wash the car, I put you in the car and had to turn it around. You thought we were going for a drive, so when I switched the car off, you would not get out. I left the door open and started washing the car, but I did not see you get out. When I looked in the back, you were sitting up there with mud throughout the car; you had gotten out, walked in the mud, jumped back in, and were glaring at me. Lesson learned.

When you were four, I thought you needed a companion to keep you company; into our lives came Shasta. I walked into the pet shop and in a pen was a litter of pure white puppies.

"What breed are they?" I asked the pet shop girl.

"Maremma puppies." She replied.

My heart melted, I would have taken all of them if I could, but one little girl with the curliest tail came home. Welcome home, Shasta.

You thought she was ok and tolerated her as long as she understood that you were boss. As the years rolled by, Shasta grew into a beautiful, big-white girl; such a gentle soul and you loved us both. We were your flock to look after, care for, and to protect.

When Kanook was cranky with me, he would go down the back stairs and get in his kennel. Poor Shasta. She would go down and lay in front of his kennel and then run upstairs to check on me. I could see the look on her face. She was saying, you two make up so I can protect you both in one place.

Shasta, your happy place was on the couch with Kanook and me. Then you started having what I called sleep terrors, where you would thrash around in your sleep. Kanook was horrified and would leave the room. As the years rolled on, your sleep terrors gradually got worse, and nobody had answers for me. Your blood tests were normal. The vet said just leave her be, she isn't in any pain, but I hated it, my poor baby girl.

The three of us would go for walks. Kanook, you loved it after it rained as there would be water in the drains, which you could walk in. But you were terrified of storms and fireworks. I am so sorry it took me so long to figure out you were not just being naughty – you were scared. But once I realised that you were scared, I never left you when there were fireworks. Sometimes I didn't have a choice with storms because I would be at work.

Through the bad times and good, you were always there for me. When my heart was broken, you would let me cry into your fur. I just didn't know that when the worst heartbreak came, you would not be beside me.

The landlord pulled our fence down, so you were both locked down in the back. It was a couple of weeks later, and I knew you were not well, so I called our vet. She came to see you and gave you some antibiotics as you had diarrhea. A few days went by, and I rang her again. She said she would drop off some more antibiotics. We still had no fence, you were locked away from me, and you hated it.

On Saturday, July 30th I went down to see you, you could hardly get up and our vet didn't work on weekends, so I rang the emergency vet. I could not get you in the car and they said they couldn't help. My son rang and asked what was wrong, when I told him, he rang the vets and lucky for us, an off-duty vet with the van was in to do some gardening. He came and took one look at you and said you were very sick and took you away, he said to give him until the afternoon to do some tests. Shasta screamed when they took you and I was crying.

I went to see you just after lunch. The tests didn't show anything other than your liver was enlarged. I cuddled you, but the light was gone from your eyes, you were ill, so ill. They had you on pain relievers and strong antibiotics.

On Sunday morning I went to see you to bring your blankie, as I thought you would be coming home with me. When they bought you in, you couldn't even wag your tail. We took you outside, the vet held your back end up with a towel. We went back in and she brought in some chicken to see if you would eat something. You just laid your head in my lap refusing to eat. The vet did not know what was wrong but she said suspected you had cancer of the bowel.

I asked her if Kanook was her dog, what would she do. She said she'd put him to sleep. Bawling like a baby, I agreed.

I knew in my heart it was best for you. She left the room to get everything needed. I stepped over you as by this time you didn't have the strength to sit up. You raised your head and looked at me.

"I'm not leaving you, buddy." I laid down behind you as you relaxed your body into mine. I cried into your fur for the last time that morning; you would not be coming home with me. My heart was broken, you were not there to comfort me as you had so many times, and now I had to go home and tell Shasta girl – she was heartbroken. Every night she would drag your bed down to the gate to sleep on.

We still had no fence. Five weeks without a fence, I was so angry. Maybe if you were with me, I could have noticed your illness sooner. Eventually, we finally got the fence up and Shasta was back up in the house.

I walked into the house one evening after work, Shasta behind me and when I turned around, there you were standing behind Shasta just like you had a million times before. I felt happy knowing you were still with me but also broken. As the months progressed, I could not stop crying and missing you. Many times I cried into your soft fur, Shasta, but you were grieving as well, you would walk through the house crying and whimpering for our boy.

Finally, I made a Reiki appointment to help me with my grief. On Saturday, March 3rd, 2017, I went and had my Reiki session. I left there feeling lighter than I had since you left.

A couple of hours later, I got a text message. All it said was, *Goodbye*. My brother-in-law sent it to me and then hung himself.

Shasta, you were there for me to cry into your fur this time. Somehow, I got through that and our lives went on, you and me, big girl, just you and me now.

Christmas 2018, I noticed you had a lump in your mouth. The vet examined you, but she found you had a row of tumours on both sides of your mouth. She said to just watch you, but your tumours grew and you would bite them when you were having your sleep terrors. I took a couple of weeks off work and made the appointment on April 11th. That morning we made you comfortable on your blankie. The vet was crying, I was crying, and I said my last goodbye to you. As your heart stopped, I knew our boy was there to take you home. No more pain, no more heartache, you could run free with our Cookie once again. I miss you both so much.

When my mum passed away suddenly on July 10th, there was no fur to cry into, no one to lick the tears from my face, no one to hold - my heart was broken into a million pieces. I could not take it anymore, but I had to make sure my dad was ok. He too passed just six months later in January 2019.

This is our story of the unconditional love you both gave me every day. It never will be equaled, never be forgotten; you live on in my heart. I miss you both every day and I always seem to be crying for one or both of you, and sometimes I even cry for myself. They say when you feel the pain in your heart, it is your past dog wagging his tail. Well, you two sure do wag your tails a lot. My heart and soul dogs, we will meet again one day. I love you both.
Your forever mum,
Sharon

Kanook

Shasta

Sebastian the Goldendoodle, My Four-Legged Angel
By Susana Saldivar

Sebastian was meant to be with me. The way he came into my life was unique. I tried two different breeders. With the first puppy, we didn't have the same personality. She was very active and needed a bigger space. The second time, I was about to get the puppy, but he got sick, and the breeder canceled the contract. Searching, I found Sebastian's breeder. I got in contact with her, and she sent me pictures of "my" puppy. Then, the day I went to pick him up, she gave me Sebastian, and she told me that he was not the puppy in the pictures she sent me. She told me that she had sold him to somebody else and she was giving me his brother. I got a little upset thinking, why was she giving me a different puppy? But I didn't care. As soon as I saw Sebastian, I fell in love with him; that was love at first sight. I feel he also bonded with me that day. He was precious. He came into my life when I was feeling lonely.

I was not working due to a car accident I had months before, so the first year I was lucky to spend day and night with him.

My main concern was potty training, but Sebastian was the best puppy ever. He was so easy to train and never had an accident in the house like he already knew what to do, it was incredible.

As the days passed, he got more confident and playful. He followed me everywhere, but he started throwing tantrums, especially when it was walking time. He would lay on the street and not want to move, he would try to "attack" me. Being playful one night, I started "crying" on the street thinking he didn't love me, people would stop by and ask me if I needed help, that was funny and embarrassing. After that episode, it was like he was a different puppy. He became so loving and listened to most of the things I asked him to do; he also understood my sadness and frustration.

I took him to puppy training, but we didn't continue with the training because he would just lay on the floor and not do anything, it was frustrating but at the same time it was funny.

He was playful, going to the park, car rides, stuffed toys, he loved it all.

He also helped my family heal. He helped my younger sister and nephew overcome their fear of dogs, like a therapy dog. My younger sister was afraid of dogs since she was little, it continued as she was an adult, and she passed the fear to her son. When Sebastian came to the family, he would approach them carefully like he knew about their fear and little by little he healed them. One day my nephew was petting him without noticing, he was not afraid.

Sebastian was a special dog, he came into my life to heal me; I was suffering from eating disorders, anxiety, and feeling lonely. He came to fill my life with joy, and he showed me the true meaning of unconditional love - he helped me to accept myself without any judgment.

Sebastian taught me to slow down and take it easy, as he had a very calming and soothing presence around me, always cuddling and snuggling me.

He was like an old soul that came to be here with me, and if he had human speech, we probably would be talking about how wonderful life is and enjoying the finer things in life. He had a sense of really appreciating everything that was going on around him; I even think he was plotting how to carefully move at a very definite pace to teach me to slow down and take it easy.

I was very busy, trying to do everything at once, and my nervous system would get all wrapped up. Sebastian's presence was very soothing and calming around me, and he taught me how to enjoy life.

He was the kind of dog that loved the outdoors. He loved when we drove around the countryside, enjoying the new views with the windows down. We walked every day, but he was not the kind of dog that loved exercise, he had the ability to exercise, but he seemed to love the sense of stillness and peace. He was very loyal and faithful.

Sebastian was protective of everything that had value to him in a loving way; protective of me, his toys, his feeding bowls, and my family, especially my parents. When my friend would visit, he would be so happy that he didn't want them to leave.

He loved nature, good music, and food—beautiful and comfortable things. He was an affectionate dog, fervent kisser, and very mild-mannered. He protected his humans; when he sensed there was danger, he would move quickly.

He loved his routine, though. He'd claim his place on the bed and knew that after his walks, I'd give him his treats, and he would wait patiently.

He perceived what was going on around, he was very intuitive, I noticed he would pick up on whatever I was thinking. For instance, sometimes when I was going out and I was thinking about taking him, without me telling him a word, he already knew. He would run to the door and wait for me to put his harness on, it was impressive. I would ask him how he knew I was going to take him with me.

He loved companionship and was happy with people around him. He wanted to take care of his humans; he was sweet and nurturing. If he felt he was being useful, it made him happier. He just wanted to please.

I believe that part of his identity was very much tied into grounding awareness in me to have compassion and sensitivity to other people and myself too. I felt he picked up that I was very self-critical and held myself back; he would come around and remind me that I am wonderful and not to be so hard on myself. He motivated me to be myself and take a risk. He was a dog that I could trust - I felt free as he loved me unconditionally. There was mutual caring between us. Sebastian wanted to be the big kid, to play and enjoy every moment in life.

His passing was sudden and unexpected. He started having seizures in May 2019. At the ER, the neurologist performed an MRI, which didn't show anything of concern, he was fine, and I did everything to help him. I consulted with a holistic vet, and we tried changing his diet and supplements. We were optimistic and had faith the seizures could be controlled. Then seven months later, in December, his health declined suddenly. I took him to the ER, where they kept him overnight. I remember promising to come back for him the next day and take him home. Little did I know that it was the last time I would see him alive. The vet called me in the morning to let me know his health was declining, and he was not sure if he would make it. I didn't get there in time to be with my boy. He passed before I got there.

The neurologist did a post-mortem MRI which showed a brain tumor occupying a quarter of his brain, apparently it was an aggressive tumor that grew over a seven-month period.

I could not believe my beloved Sebastian was gone. Seven months later, I still cannot believe it. How I wish my boy was back here with me, I miss him every single day.

After his passing I was so sad, crying every day and night, holding tightly to his toys as I slept. I would dream about him. Even my cats felt sadness, one of them was depressed for about a month, she would come every night and lay next to me.

I know he wouldn't want to see me like this, I have tried everything in my power to try to be myself, but I know that without him I won't be complete, a part of my heart is missing.

The way I am trying to heal is by getting close to God, scrapbooking with his pictures, creating a memorial garden, and I have pictures of him on my phone case, laptop, everywhere. With pieces of his hair, I had made some jewelry. Now I have him close to my heart.

I never imagined his passing would be so painful. He taught me to take care of my body and to value life and my loved ones because we never know what tomorrow may bring. Sebastian was my soul dog.

I know he is still nurturing me from heaven, and he is by my side. He will never let me be alone.

Sebastian